Japanese Color Matching

sendpoints

Japanese Color Matching

Third printing of the first edition, August 2025

sendpoints

PUBLISHED BY SendPoints Publishing Co., Ltd.
ADDRESS: Unit 23, L1/F Mirror Tower, 61 Mody Road, Tsim Sha Tsui, Kowloon, Hong Kong, China
PUBLISHER: Lin Gengli
PUBLISHING DIRECTOR: Nicole Lo
CHIEF EDITOR: Nicole Lo
EXECUTIVE EDITOR: Zeng Wanting
COVER ILLUSTRATOR: Eriko Kawakami (JP)
EXECUTIVE ART EDITOR: Peng Zhenwei Design Office
TRANSLATOR: Xu Yuxiao
PROOFREADERS: Huang Chujun, Zeng Wanting, Beijing Chinese-Foreign Translation & Information Service Co., Ltd. Joseph Taplin

SALES DIRECTOR: Philip Tsang
TEL: +852 6296 2246
EMAIL: sales@sppub.com
WEBSITE: www.sppub.com

ISBN 978-988-76087-9-0

Printed and bound in China.

Facebook

Instagram

X

CONTENTS

Preface

Japan · Color

In Japan, men and women, young and old dress themselves in various colors and styles. You can find young ladies dressed in traditional kimonos, office workers in formal suits, girls wearing elaborate maid outfits, rebellious teenagers with dark, gothic makeup, citizens dressed casually and even cosplayers in intricate costumes attending anime conventions... The fashion elements in Japan are so diverse and extreme that they would hardly appear at the same time and location in other countries, yet the streets of Japan seemingly exist as a veritable "melting pot of colors" to the point that one is unphased by its presence.

The Japanese as a people group have well-defined emotions and a sharp eye for colors. They like to inject their own values and attitudes into their colors, endowing them with emotions and personality. Gradually, color has come to be a cultural symbol, deeply related to public psychology and social ideology. It reflects differences in age, gender, hobby, status and personality and is revealed in every aspect of life.

Having affection for both plain and bright colors, Japanese people opt for a wide color gamut and rich hues. They excel at using colors to display their unique national and personal aesthetics and cultural values. These styles range from retro colors that have prevailed for half a century and minimalistic colors with modern characteristics, to Kawaii colors suitable for all ages and bizarre color matching schemes that are avant-garde in nature.

Starting from these 4 main styles: retro style, minimalism, Kawaii and avant-garde, this book categorizes popular Japanese color schemes and aims to provide a broad overview of how color origins, cultural values and color features have influenced Japanese contemporary aesthetics. It also discusses how the Japanese use colors to embody their emotions and the ways in which color schemes are used for visual enjoyment. In this book, a wide range of color schemes and a systematic color atlas will empower the reader to better understand popular Japanese colors and can serve as inspiration for making one's own unique color scheme!

Contemporary Color Trends in Japan

The formation of color styles and its trends have undergone a complete process of development. As one of the first East Asian countries to be exposed to modern popular culture from Europe and the US, Japan is a cradle for design styles and trends that are most representative of Asia.

Japan is nation that is particularly fond of colors. Through the integration of local Japanese culture and globalization, 4 classic Japanese-style color schemes have come into being. These schemes, born in Japan and popularized throughout Asia, embody the lifestyles and fashion tastes of contemporary Japanese trendsetters. They serve as the sources of inspiration for professional designers in their pursuit of aesthetics.

Retro Sense　Minimalism　Kawaii　Avant-garde

終わらないクラ
Classics That Never Fade
シック
→
レトロノスタル
Retro Nostalgia
ジア

Poster of *Humanity and Paper Balloons*, 1937
Source: Shochiku Company, Toho Company (Wikimedia)

四天王寺

東洲齋寫

寫楽画

Poster of *Tokyo Story*, 1953
Source: Shochiku Company (Wikimedia)

The Heisei Period (1989—2019) has given way to the Reiwa Period (2019—) in Japan. Now the retro style of the period before Heisei, known as the Showa Period (1926—1989), is on the rise. This retro trend is spreading nationwide across Japan and has had an impact on more than a few small shops, which are now adopting Showa era décor and selling nostalgic goods and souvenirs. There are other spaces besides stores putting this period on display. The Hida Takayama Retro Museum has exhibited a great number of objects that were in use between 1945 and 1975; Nagoya has recreated school canteens in the 1950s; and mini retro home appliances referred to as "The Showa Series" were on display at a household items fair...

The Showa Period is considered to be a golden age in Japan. It spanned almost the entire reign of Hirohito from 1926 to 1989. The Showa Retro Style usually refers to retro designs modelled after objects from the 1950s to 1970s. This trend has been steadily gaining ground since the 1990s. Young Japanese people, facing serious issues as Japan becomes an aged society, live and work under great pressure. As a result, they have stopped actively seeking out novelty or excitement, preferring instead to soothe anxieties by looking back into the past. The peaceful grandeur of the Showa Period has gradually become attractive. Thus, designs that reflect this period have become increasingly popular among the Japanese.

Objects containing design elements of the Showa Retro Style are everywhere in Japan, including old movie posters in the streets, old-fashioned shops with nostalgic decorations, buildings featuring Showa-era architecture, ubiquitous vintage clothing stores, and women's make-up and clothes mimicking this 20th century style. The shapes and designs of these objects are rooted in the aesthetics of the Showa era, and the saturation and sharpness of their colors are lowered to resemble the period more closely.

Designs are made for our future, and our future requires we inherit our historical relics. We need to make designs based on the past to remember to ensure we don't lose what we have.

TAKU SATOH

Compared with the Showa Retro Style, Amekaji is another retro style that is even more popular. Amekaji originated from American casual styles as seen in the 1940s to 1960s. When the American style spread to Japan in the 1990s, it was adjusted and adapted by the Japanese. Having been integrated with the local culture, the American retro casual style merged with Japanese characteristics. Amekaji mainly prevails in the fashion world and can be seen in the form of biker jackets, overalls, military uniforms and jeanswear. Its most distinctive feature is its amazing charm as a replica. The colors for this clothing style are either nostalgic and classic or simple and elegant. Either way, the style invokes a sense of antiquity. Amekaji is now incredibly popular among Japanese young people, especially trendsetters.

Apart from these 2 retro styles that are marked by the distinct features of their times, many other items in Japan likewise follow this retro approach in a less obvious way. Despite their international and modern appearance, they are actually retro in nature judging by their color matching. Their quotidian design causes people to easily overlook the unique Japanese elements embedded in these objects primarily via color. Examples of this include lacquerware, vessels and buildings that are black and red in color; blue and white clothing, posters and tenugui (a cloth for wiping one's hands); red and white wedding clothes and holiday gifts. Regardless of the design, a distinctly retro Japanese style can be created by combining the 4 most nostalgic colors white, black, red and blue. The next step is to reduce the brightness of the colors or increase their gray scale. A rule of retro style color matching, albeit not an absolute but frequently applied rule, can even be inferred from the above practices: An atmosphere that is serious, classic, tranquil or desolate can be constructed by juxtaposing the 4 colors with other duller ones. Utilizing this "rule", designers create different atmospheres to present the nostalgia for Japan's rich culture and history.

US overalls in the 1940s
Source: U.S. Naval History and Heritage Command (Wikimedia)

Source: Taimichi, Retro Stationery Collector

I think designs are like water flowing from different sources. They are distinguished by their places of origin. These designs in turn become features of the places where they are from.

SHOGO KISHINO

NEW DRAWING PENCILS
HARRIS
PENCILS
MARS
A.W. FABER "JANUS"
PREIS-MEDAILLEN
A.W. FABER
ZEICHNEN-REQUISITEN
Die Fabrik besteht seit 1761.
STABILO
クミアイ
鉛筆
"MITSU-BISHI"
No. 727
AIRPORT
BLACK
MARKING PENCILS
日本海海戰
MADE IN ENGLAND
"British Drawing"
CUMBERLAND PENCIL Co. LTD
一三菱試驗用

Source: Taimichi, Retro Stationery Collector

色が崩れるシック

Less Is More

ク

Minimal Colors

ミニマリズムか

らアドバンスト

Lump-Bowl for Urushi Kobo Oshima
Studio: Kuroyanagi Jun Design Hut
Designer: nendo
Photographer: Akihiro Yoshida

Ryogen-in of Daitoku-ji in Kyoto, Japan

We wish to present this minimalist design, but not in such a streamlined way that the design loses its warmth. The design I want to achieve has a human touch as it links people and objects and presents the humor or surprise embedded in everyday life.

—

OKI SATO

Cluttered, disorderly, crude, rough... These words once could describe the homes of most young people. Today, however, the younger generation has begun to pursue a higher quality of life and more sophisticated living environments. Despite Japan's economic conditions, they still keep their spaces tidy and create a sense of sophistication attainable by ordinary people to show their love and desire for their lives. For example, Marie Kondo, a popular organizational expert, has transformed herself from an ordinary housewife to an Internet celebrity and best-selling author by introducing various organizing methods. There have been a plethora of books, TV shows and online streaming content about organizing and tidying emerging. The minimalist lifestyle is the new trend. From household decor and clothing to products and design, all aspects of life are trending toward minimalism. Although it may appear as though this minimalist approach is solely focused on reducing the amount of things one owns, it actually reveals people's ideal for living a refined and sophisticated life within one's means.

Looking back at Japan in the 1970s and 1980s when its economy was booming, people were well off and enjoyed abundant forms of entertainment. Flamboyant and bright colors were the new trend at the time. This all changed with the country's bubble economy of the late 1980s and early 1990s. The economy took a major hit. Gone were the days of prosperity. People's lives changed as well. Economic pressures forced them to part with some unnecessary household items, leading to practicality and simplicity becoming the new trend. Now a luxurious life was replaced with one marked by simplicity. The gaudy taste was set aside for elegance.

WonderLand, 1973

WonderLand, 1973

Source: MUJI

Today, the Japanese view of sophistication is always associated with nature and minimalism, which can be traced back to ancient Japanese styles of landscape painting and architecture. However, this is distinct from the retro style. Japanese minimalist design retains its national and religious characteristics, with an aesthetic trend of being cool, pure and simple, which was created under the strong influence of Zen Buddhism. Nature is everywhere. There are many ways to create a sense of sophistication, and one of the most simple and direct ones is to choose the right colors. On the one hand, compared with a Scandinavian style that mainly uses black, white and gray, the Japanese minimalist style is usually based on a natural wood color to reflect the essence of nature; the matching colors also tend to be soft, restrained, plain, fresh and elegant. After mixing, the color becomes more neutral, going from pure white to beige. On the other hand, low contrast, saturation or value also aids in creating a pure and mysterious visual impression. Colors that are more minimal and streamlined depict a greater sense of quiet sophistication. Additionally, lower saturation and higher grayscale also help to highlight that sophistication.

Japanese designers are well-versed in practicing this use of natural colors to depict a sense of sophistication. One prime example of this is MUJI. MUJI's philosophy of simplicity and elegance and its return to nature strongly aligns with Japanese Zen Buddhism and minimalism, and it has applied this philosophy to all aspects of the

Advanced design should be done in such a way that you don't sense its presence. When the object is in front of you, you naturally won't think it's specifically designed, but before long you'll come to realize the ingenuity of its designer. That kind of subtle design is a master-level design.

—

KENYA HARA

company, including store décor and product design. MUJI uses white, beige and natural wood colors as its main hues, which confer a greater sense of its product design and the décor as quiet, delicate, and light when compared to the colorful and dazzling products seen in other stores. MUJI maintains a sense of texture and original beauty, while its simple and understated color scheme surprisingly belies a sense of elegance and nobility.

"Less is more" has become the norm. Whether in daily life, corporate branding, or personal lifestyle, people tend to avoid using too many design elements or colors. The more elements and brighter the colors used, the easier it is to give the impression of flamboyance as well as a sense of inferiority. Conversely, neutral colors and earthy tones with a light sense of indifference look much cleaner. Therefore, by reducing excessive decorations, minimalism has become a new, classy aesthetic in modern life.

Galleria Akka in Osaka, Japan
Architect: Tadao Ando
Source: Oiuysdfg (Wikimedia)

TINT
Studio: UMA/Design Farm
Designer: Yuka Tsuda
Art Director: Yuma Harada
Photographer: Yoshiro Masuda

TSUMIKI Stacking Blocks
Studio: More Trees Design, Inc.
Designer: Kengo Kuma
Photographers: Ikunori Yamamoto, Keisuke Ono

We talk a lot about "added value". But since it has become an expectation, I think we are seeing too many products and services derived from it that are basically meaningless.

TAKU SATOH

ナショナルCプ

The National Favorite

レイス

→

カワイイ

Kawaii

PIE

The most influential and representative style in Japan by far is the Kawaii (or cute) style, which is popular among almost all age groups. This style, however, has only a short history. In the 1960s, the anime, music, cartoon film and video game industries began to develop in Japan. Although the Kawaii style, which was derived from these industries, is now one of the quintessential elements of Japanese pop culture, back then those cultural industries were not very popular. In the 1980s, the economic growth of post-WWII Japan brought people wonderful forms of entertainment and added a splash of color to their lives. But it was quickly replaced by the bursting of the bubble economy in the 1990s that resulted in a decade-long recession and subsequently cast a pall over all of Japan due to the stark difference. As the times grew darker, more people pursued light; the heavier the social atmosphere, the more eager people were to reach out toward cute and sweet things.

For Japanese people, fierce competition can be found at every corner, from school to the workplace. A culture of cuteness within the context of this strict and serious social

Manga series *Astro Boy* (Japanese: 鉄腕アトム), April 1952–March 1968
Manga Artist: Osamu Tezuka
Source: Atom.D (Flickr)

Manga series *Dragon Ball* (Japanese: ドラゴンボール), 1984–1995
Manga Artist: Toriyama Akira
Source: Instacodez (Flickr)

I think the strong red color and the simplicity from using colored pencils express my ideas better.

KAZUMASA NAGAI

atmosphere offers a potent conduit for people to relieve their anxiety and stress. Caught in a monotonous and high-pressure life, people long for mental relaxation and pleasure, and the light and sweet culture of Kawaii provides that very escape. Today, modern young people live well-off lives, so they have moved away from the materialistic pursuit based on the practical sensibilities of the 20th century to a higher level of spiritual contentment. Now, they prioritize their psychological needs. Even as people grow up and enter their middle years, they still wish to retain their desire for the carefree and innocent life of their childhoods. This is a key reason behind the development and prevalence of Kawaii culture in Japan.

In other countries, cuteness is thought to be childish, frivolous and weak. In Japan, however, this style is not limited to women and children. It can also be found in formal contexts, such as government publications, public notice boards, corporate images and exhibition guides. Kawaii has even given rise to a variety of other subcultures, such as otaku culture, ACG culture and cuteness (referred to as Meng in China) culture. Hello Kitty, Pikachu, Doraemon, Ultraman, Kumamoto Bear and other cute ACG Japanese characters have even gone beyond Japan's borders to enjoy a global reputation. This all-round penetration and development not only represent a fashion trend, but also fully reflect the unique aesthetic as well as the great charm and appeal of modern Japanese subculture.

Whether one is discussing graphic design, mascot design, anime character design or product design, Kawaii derivatives are generally cute and lively in style, featuring colorful, soft or sweet tones. A pink tone and warm colors of high value or high brightness combine to create a happy and joyful atmosphere.

Suddenly, "a primary school, a man walking with his dog, and an old man riding a bicycle" all come into my sight, and my mind would go "Ah". Moments or chances like this happen, and they have ineffable charm to me.

—

KAZUNARI HATTORI

Pikachu
Source: GT#2...thanks for millionth support (Flickr)

Hello Kitty Lanterns
Source: Miki Yoshihito (Wikimedia)

Hello Kitty Theme Cafe
Source: othree (Wikimedia)

Free, outgoing, interesting, and cheerful. Although I want to become such a person, I am not that type at all. So, I want to experiment with things that are free and interesting when it comes to graphic design.

KAZUNARI HATTORI

I think we have many beautiful, cool and cute designs in Japanese graphic design.

MANABU MIZUNO

ニッチなデザ

Other Non-mainstream Designs

イン

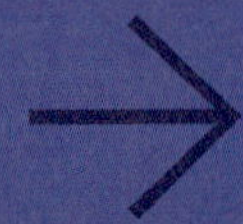

新世代、

New Generation

新色、

New Color Scheme

新人格

New Characters

Waka Graphics
Studio: AYOND
Designer: Shun Sasaki

Though there are objects and designs in the styles of Kawaii style or minimalism, or the fresh style everywhere in Japan, the pursuit of individuality by young Japanese people has spurred the rise of another non-mainstream wave. Influenced by pop cultures such as punk and rock in Europe and the US, some avant-garde and adventurous designs and color schemes have come into vogue among young people in Japan. Goth and "New Ugly" represent relatively more extreme examples of the trend. Although these various styles have their unique characteristics, they all belong to Japan's street culture.

Aesthetic fatigue inevitably creeps in when one is surrounded by the lovely Kawaii style for a long time. A new generation grew bored of past fashion, leading to a change in color style preferences in Japan. The new generation's rebellious nature is reflected through many different types of fashion, including the dark Gothic look in fashion circles and unconventional "Ugly" designs in graphic design circles.

Derived from British fashion, the Goth style prevailed for a time in the 1970s and was introduced to Japan in the 1980s, when it integrated with local punk elements. Japanese Gothic fashion is mainly gloomy, strange and mysterious. Most of its colors are cold in tone, with black being the color of choice. Black, unadorned by any other color, can express the strongest sense of individuality. After Goth's initial introduction, its dark aesthetics interweaved with the local Loli culture, resulting in visual art unique to Japan -- the Gothic Lolita. Besides retaining the gloom and decadence of Gothic fashion, Gothic Lolita also kept the elegance and gorgeousness of Japan's Lolita. These features produced a dark, strange, melancholy and mysterious characteristic. The style is mainly expressed in clothing, anime and manga, featuring elements such as Victorian panoplies, roses, crosses, lace, falbalas, ribbons, dolls and maid outfits. Its color tones are usually black and white.

Another style is called "New Ugly". Its inception happened later than Japanese Gothic fashion, but it is similar as it is also a highly individualized style. "New Ugly" is usually applied to graphic designs. Even though it has little to do with the Japanese Gothic look, perhaps even existing as its polar opposite, the 2 styles share a similar spirit, which is rebelling against the status quo.

Nobody wants to do something boring .

MANABU MIZUNO

Poster *Brain*
Designer: Hirano Kouga

It is like putting on the top and the bottom, then packing it up nicely. This is a typical pictographic character.

Poster *Sceret*
Designer: Hirano Kouga

Poster *Sky*
Designer: Hirano Kouga

Poster *The Heart Sutra*
Designer: Hirano Kouga

From the late 20th century to early 21st century, the steady proliferation of street ads, diner menus, independent publications, etc. drew attention from the design community. Influenced by punk culture, brutalism and critical graphic design, such seemingly vulgar designs were intense, absurd and rough, a kaleidoscope of every ridiculous element that lacked any visible convention. Mainstream designers believed this approach lacked design and was an affront to the eyes. However, designers working with these new concepts saw the style as a different aesthetic expression and products of said style were considered refreshing. In those emerging designs, symmetry and framework were purposely broken; typefaces were stretched and twisted. Irrationality was fused into retro and gaudy styles with characteristically psychedelic colors and unconventional layouts. This chaotic mashing together of elements brought forth a genuinely revolutionary "New Ugly" aesthetic. Artists and designers in "New Ugly" aim to integrate rough, brutal and primitive designs into the mundane minutiae of life. They spurn authorities and standards, pursuing critical introspection that leans toward avant-garde aesthetics. Further, they make every effort to incorporate their self-awareness into their designs to explore a new world that is overlooked by modern designs. They hope people spend time observing and understanding things rather than making unconscious judgment of beauty or ugliness; they want to bring consumers of these designs into a deeper level of participation with the content and have them be impacted by the postmodern "Ugly". Each design in "New Ugly" differs from the next as there are no universal rules nor such a thing as sheer beauty or ugliness. The prevalence of "New Ugly" designs and the rise of such a divergence are at its root a redefinition of beauty and ugliness and a rebellion of the former against established rules.

This type of unusual and revolutionary aesthetic differs from what can be considered an orthodox color scheme. Its seemingly gaudy colors with high brightness and saturation precisely represents the perplexity and rebellion of the young generation in modern Japan, a group expressing their aesthetic preference of defying authorities and standards and pursuing avant-garde as well as their individuality that leads to self-awareness.

The works of Tadanori Yokoo uncovered the unbearable things lurking within the Japanese people. These are the things frustrating us and instilling us with fear. He used such gaudy and extreme colors — it's an impolite art. Unlike the world of madmen twisting inward over and over again, Yokoo created an inclusive and absurd world that unfolds before everyone's eyes, and it was such inclusiveness and craziness that his works have turned into something positive.

YUKIO MISHIMA

A LA MAISON DE M. CIVEÇAWA / US Garumera Chamber of Commerce in Ankuku Butoh school / 1965
1030 mm × 728 mm / MoMA
Artist: Tadanori Yokoo

Koshimaki-osen / Condition Troupe / 1030 mm × 728 mm / MoMA / 1966
Artist: Tadanori Yokoo

TADANORI YOKOO, A poster that Tadanori Yokoo designed for himself
Artist: Tadanori Yokoo

If there's any adventurous tone or abstract sign in my works, that's because I always pursue the creation of something unforgettable.

KASHIWA SATO

Red, green, blue... Those primary colors have no meaning in and of themselves, but they can magically trigger resonance and leave similar visual impressions among different people through ingenious design. They can gradually create a unique color style. The Japanese have such great interest in color that they have widely applied their highly-valued color scheme not only in their designs, but also throughout daily life. With diverse ideas and designs, they strive to spread a color style that is emblematic of Japanese culture all over the world.

Projects

*Color values are for reference only.

レトロセンス
Retro Sense

Chapter

○ A sense of luxury with the color gold/ ○ Lovely and retro/ ○ Low brightness × Pink/ ○ Surreal geometric color blocks/ ○ Matching color with flavor/ ○ Traditional Japanese black and red/ ○ The classic festive color scheme/ ○ Using classic black and red to highlight Japan's national character/ ○ Light pink for creating a retro style/ ○ Colors match the product characteristics/ ○ Deliberately using old tones/ ○ Colors correlate with local culture and things/ ○ Comparison between schemes and formats/ ○ Matching colors and lines/ ○ A classic combination of black, white and gold/ ○ Achieve a sense of balance through color matching/ ○ Simple composition and color matching create a strong effect/ ○ Cultural inheritance in storefront design/ ○ Japanese Kyoto style revealed through colors/ ○ Monochrome colors that gradually change color/ ○ Achieve the best effects with the simplest colors/ ○ Integrating modern natural features with Edo period styles

01

Hakuichi's 40th Anniversary Brochure

Art Director: Yoichi Hisamatsu
Illustrator: Kazuya Yamashita

C:68 M:6 Y:65 K:0
R:76 G:175 B:119

C:0 M:98 Y:70 K:0
R:230 G:14 B:57

C:18 M:30 Y:55 K:0
R:216 G:183 B:124

C:0 M:28 Y:10 K:0
R:248 G:204 B:209

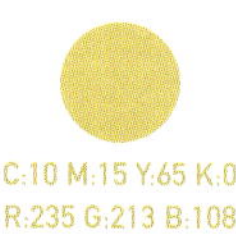

C:10 M:15 Y:65 K:0
R:235 G:213 B:108

Idea: A sense of luxury with the color gold

Hakuichi is a Japanese paper manufacturer. Made of oil-absorbing sheets with gold foil, these brochures were designed for its 40th anniversary exhibition. The female figures on the brochures wear different colored kimonos for a retro and luxurious look.

C:11 M:14 Y:45 K:0
R:233 G:217 B:155

C:77 M:0 Y:76 K:0
R:0 G:172 B:102

C:50 M:0 Y:8 K:0
R:128 G:205 B:231

C:0 M:66 Y:77 K:0
R:238 G:118 B:59

C:83 M:3 Y:24 K:0
R:0 G:169 B:195

C:17 M:31 Y:61 K:0
R:218 G:181 B:111

C:64 M:12 Y:24 K:0
R:87 G:176 B:191

C:95 M:88 Y:38 K:0
R:35 G:58 B:110

C:11 M:28 Y:55 K:0
R:230 G:191 B:125

C:56 M:63 Y:18 K:0
R:132 G:105 B:152

C:100 M:32 Y:22 K:0
R:0 G:127 B:174

C:5 M:99 Y:83 K:0
R:223 G:13 B:43

箔一
HAKUICHI
きれいは、つみ重なる。一枚ずつ。
箔一
ふるや紙
金箔打紙製法
40th
箔一 ふるや紙
HAKUICHI
FURUYAGAMI

きれいは、つみ重なる。
いまや女性になくてはならないあぶらとり紙。
その先がけともいえる「箔一のふるや紙」が誕生して
ことしで40周年を迎えました。
かつて金箔づくりの工程で使われた箔打ち紙が
肌のあぶらもとれる〝ふるや紙〟となって粋人を魅了した時代から、
箔一は、その紙を誰もが手に入れられ、
肌にやさしい安心の品質へと変えてきました。
そして、その女性のためのモノづくりの精神はこれからも。
わたしたちは紙一枚のヨロコビをつみ重ね、
美しくありたいすべての女性たちと歩んでいきます。
40th
箔一 ふるや紙
金箔打紙製法
ふるや紙

40th
箔一 ふるや紙
ふるや紙への想い
1枚ずつお使いいただけます。
ご自由にお試しください。

02

Medeta Kibidango

Studio: Cochae
Photographers: Create UNION, Masayoshi Kusai

Idea: Lovely and retro

This set of wrapping paper for millet dumplings referred to as kibi dango features the theme of "joy". When unfolded, it becomes origami paper, which has a long history in Japanese culture. There are 5 different designs, each related to a representative animal in traditional Japanese culture, such as cranes, turtles, cats and fish. For each animal, the designer chose an appropriate and lovely color scheme that is not overly bright, thus maintaining a retro style.

C:16 M:22 Y:58 K:0
R:222 G:198 B:122

C:0 M:75 Y:85 K:0
R:235 G:97 B:42

C:0 M:10 Y:100 K:0
R:255 G:225 B:0

C:70 M:0 Y:20 K:0
R:27 G:184 B:206

C:70 M:7 Y:100 K:0
R:75 G:169 B:53

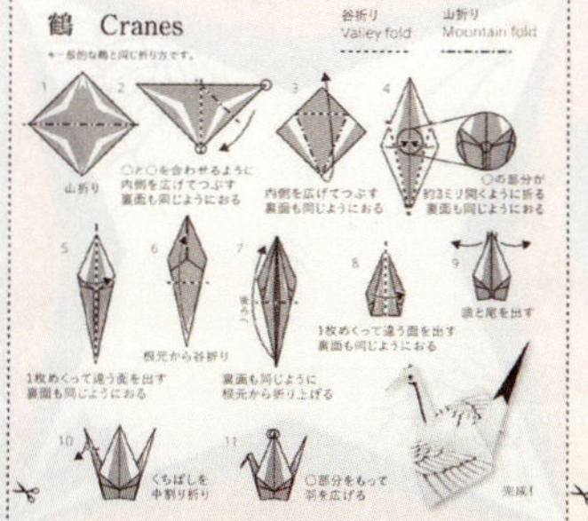

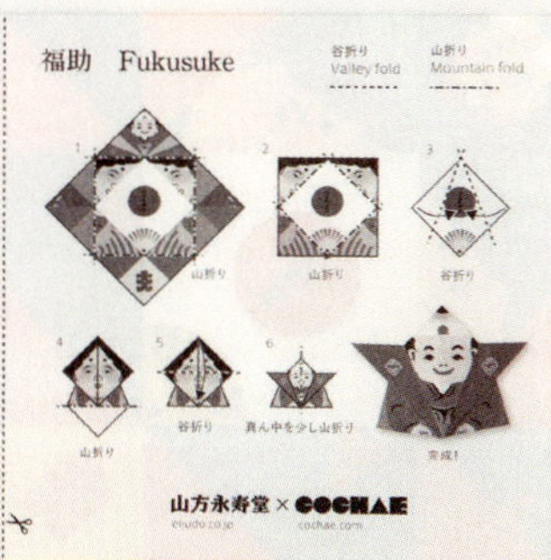

03

Folk Cartoon Storage Bag

Studio: Cochae
Photographer: Harumi Obama

Idea: Low brightness × Pink

Cochae collaborated with TOKYU HANDS to create this storage bag made from recycled paper that features folk cartoon characters. In order to show the cartoon character's folksy and cute side, a dull pink color was selected as the main color for a cute retro style.

C:0 M:92 Y:83 K:0
R:231 G:49 B:43

C:0 M:41 Y:37 K:0
R:245 G:174 B:149

C:0 M:13 Y:75 K:0
R:255 G:223 B:79

C:43 M:0 Y:18 K:0
R:153 G:212 B:215

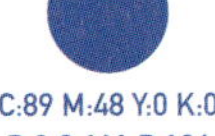

C:89 M:48 Y:0 K:0
R:0 G:111 B:186

C:45 M:80 Y:63 K:0
R:158 G:78 B:82

C:88 M:82 Y:0 K:0
R:54 G:62 B:150

C:0 M:0 Y:0 K:37
R:187 G:188 B:188

C:34 M:0 Y:44 K:0
R:182 G:218 B:165

C:62 M:0 Y:80 K:0
R:101 G:185 B:90

C:0 M:51 Y:48 K:0
R:242 G:152 B:120

C:20 M:25 Y:60 K:0
R:213 G:190 B:116

04

Su murie

Studio: Canaria Inc.
Designers: Mariko Kojima, Koji Fujii
Creative Director: Yuji Tokuda

C:5 M:8 Y:22 K:0
R:245 G:235 B:207

C:8 M:32 Y:78 K:0
R:235 G:184 B:69

C:23 M:92 Y:100 K:0
R:197 G:53 B:30

C:70 M:35 Y:100 K:0
R:92 G:137 B:52

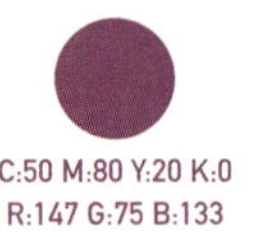
C:50 M:80 Y:20 K:0
R:147 G:75 B:133

C:10 M:55 Y:85 K:0
R:225 G:138 B:49

C:30 M:16 Y:95 K:0
R:194 G:193 B:25

C:46 M:68 Y:69 K:5
R:152 G:97 B:78

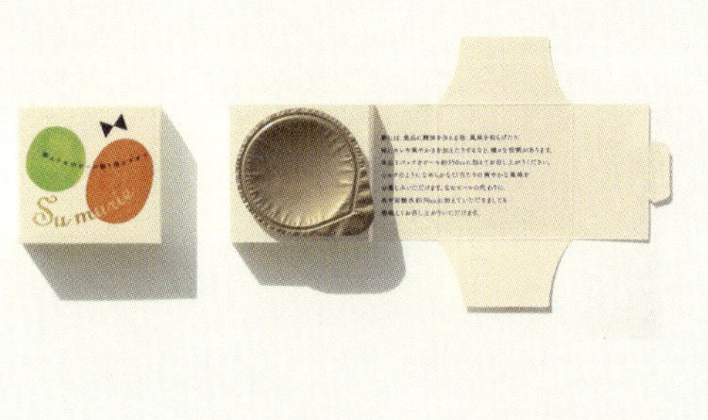

Idea: Surreal geometric color blocks

Su murie is a brand of vinegar that aims to challenge the stubborn traditional image that has affixed itself to old Japanese vinegar. The design of the packaging should retain the warmth of the brand's history while creating a new and playful atmosphere. Inspired by the works of surrealist artist Joan Miró, the design features simple, abstract geometric blocks of color in red, orange, yellow, green, cyan, blue and purple. These 2 design elements combine to create a free, light and unrestrained atmosphere that offers a touch of warmth.

Su murie

Su murie
酢ムリエのピクリングスパイス

05

Castella Packaging Design

Studio: Knot for, Inc.
Designers: Taki Uesugi, Saki Uesugi
Creative Director: Atsushi Shibuya

Idea: Matching color with flavor

This Japanese sponge cake is the product of a Nagasaki confectionery store that was established in 1900. The packaging design of the cake focuses on this city's history and culture, so it has a distinct Nagasaki style. The main color for each of the 3 packages is based on the flavor of the cake: coffee color for chocolate, light yellow for original, and bright green for matcha.

C:38 M:25 Y:85 K:0
R:175 G:174 B:65

C:46 M:77 Y:75 K:7
R:150 G:80 B:66

C:9 M:19 Y:81 K:0
R:237 G:206 B:63

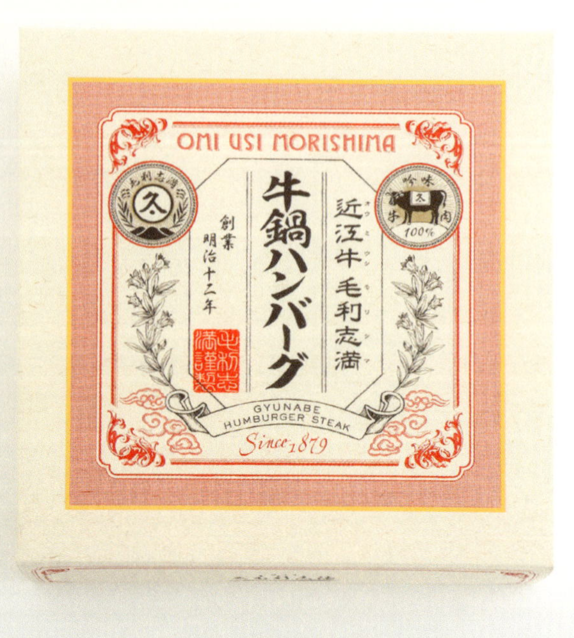
OMI USI MORISHIMA
牛鍋ハンバーグ
近江牛 毛利志満
創業
明治十二年
吟味
牛肉
100%
GYUNABE
HUMBURGER STEAK
Since 1879

OMI USI MORISHIMA
牛鍋ハンバーグ
近江牛 毛利志満
GYUNABE
HUMBURGER STEAK
Since 1879

Gyunabe Salisbury Steak Packaging Design

Studio: Knot for, Inc.
Designers: Taki Uesugi, Saki Uesugi
Photographer: Kengo Motoie

Idea: Traditional Japanese black and red

MORISHIMA is a restaurant that opened in Japan in 1879. This new package is for its Salisbury Steak. To convey the restaurant's long history, the traditional Japanese black and red were selected for the packaging. This color combination is the most representative and widely seen in Japan, with the still black and dynamic red complementing each other, thus adding a touch of fervor to solemnity.

07

New Year's Cards

Studio: Takeuma

Idea: The classic festive color scheme

This set of New Year's cards depicts the 12 zodiac signs in a minimalist design using lines and graphics. In addition, the design features the classic festive color scheme of black and red, which expresses a Japanese aesthetic in a vivid way.

C:0 M:100 Y:100 K:0
R:230 G:0 B:18

C:100 M:100 Y:100 K:100
R:0 G:0 B:0

C:0 M:55 Y:95 K:0
R:241 G:141 B:2

C:0 M:20 Y:95 K:0
R:253 G:209 B:0

08

AKOMEYA Lifestyle Brand

Studio: Knot for, Inc.
Designers: Taki Uesugi, Saki Uesugi

Idea: Using classic black and red to highlight Japan's national character

AKOMEYA TOKYO is a lifestyle grocery store that specializes in rice and delicious foods from all over Japan. Again, it uses the classic black and red color scheme for its packaging design. On a white background, black is used as the main color for graphics and text, while either red, blue or green serves as a monochromatic border. The retro graphics and simple color scheme complement each other, highlighting the brand's tradition and the weight of its history.

C:0 M:94 Y:89 K:0
R:231 G:41 B:34

C:89 M:68 Y:0 K:0
R:30 G:83 B:164

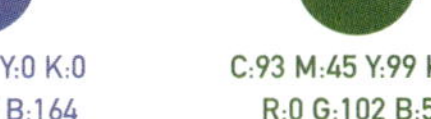

C:93 M:45 Y:99 K:15
R:0 G:102 B:55

C:25 M:31 Y:63 K:0
R:202 G:176 B:107

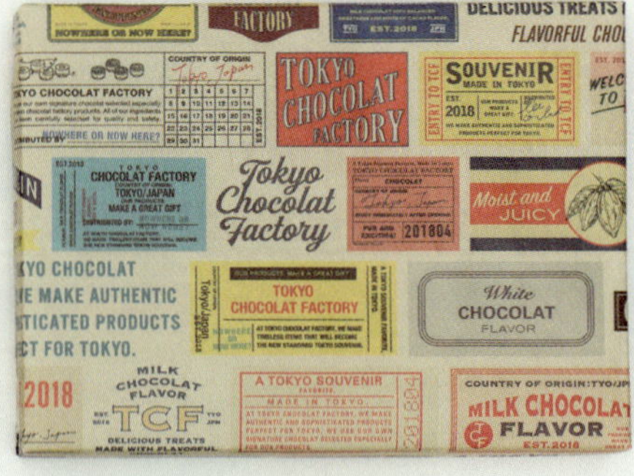

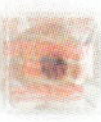

C:5 M:30 Y:18 K:0
R:239 G:196 B:192

C:20 M:19 Y:71 K:0
R:215 G:198 B:94

C:62 M:16 Y:34 K:0
R:100 G:171 B:171

C:60 M:71 Y:75 K:22
R:108 G:76 B:62

C:8 M:75 Y:58 K:0
R:223 G:96 B:87

09

TOKYO CHOCOLAT FACTORY

Studio: good design company
Creative Director: Manabu Mizuno

Idea: Light pink for creating a retro style

TOKYO CHOCOLAT FACTORY is a chocolate and candy brand in Tokyo. The theme for this design is a chocolate factory in the city. Images of factories are used in the company's logos, packaging and storefront designs. A light pink tone invokes a sense of nostalgia, and gold foil is used to highlight the brand's delicacy and quality.

10

Tea Discussion

Studio: good design company
Creative Director: Manabu Mizuno

C:75 M:75 Y:32 K:0
R:90 G:79 B:125

C:64 M:46 Y:88 K:0
R:113 G:126 B:66

Idea: Colors match the product characteristics

The traditional Japanese method of preparing and serving tea is known as tea ceremony. However, the number of people who are familiar with the tea ceremony culture is declining and is mostly comprised of the elderly. In order to attract more young people and eliminate obstacles that prevent them from knowing and accessing this traditional culture, a new brand, the Tea Discussion, was created. The concept of Tea Discussion is to "discuss the meaning of beauty through tea". The brand logo utilizes one of the most indispensable tools, the tea jar, and the text on the packaging is designed according to the most ancient tea book in Japan, Kissa Yojoki. The color scheme adopts the representative color of tea, green, and pairs it with a nostalgic mulberry.

茶
論

11 The Beauty of New Prints: The Centennial of Printmaking

Studio: Artglorieux Gallery of Tokyo
Designers: Hasui Kawase, Yasuji Inoue
Art Director: Takashi Ogawa

C:0 M:49 Y:27 K:0
R:242 G:158 B:157

C:54 M:51 Y:25 K:0
R:135 G:126 B:156

C:38 M:11 Y:78 K:0
R:175 G:195 B:84

C:81 M:36 Y:81 K:0
R:42 G:130 B:84

C:31 M:3 Y:23 K:0
R:187 G:220 B:206

C:13 M:40 Y:81 K:0
R:224 G:166 B:62

C:60 M:22 Y:28 K:0
R:109 G:166 B:177

C:10 M:65 Y:85 K:0
R:223 G:117 B:47

C:81 M:30 Y:25 K:0
R:0 G:140 B:173

C:54 M:16 Y:67 K:0
R:131 G:175 B:110

C:100 M:52 Y:82 K:18
R:0 G:90 B:70

C:7 M:20 Y:60 K:0
R:240 G:208 B:118

Idea: Deliberately using old tones

To revitalize the declining traditional Japanese art known as Ukiyo-e, Hasui Kawase took the initiative to begin a new stage for Ukiyo-e — the New Print Movement.

For this exhibition, Hasui Kawase worked with his premier printer, S. Watanabe Woodcut Print. The exhibition displays 30 prints, including Kawase's acclaimed series, *Twenty Views of Tokyo*. These prints imitate the tones of the Ukiyo-e style from the Edo period. Amateur views may mistake them for original works created hundreds of years ago.

12

Ukiyo-e

Studio: Artglorieux Gallery of Tokyo
Designers: Hasui Kawase, Yasuji Inoue
Art Director: Takashi Ogawa

C:20 M:96 Y:75 K:0
R:201 G:37 B:57

C:20 M:35 Y:35 K:0
R:210 G:175 B:157

C:44 M:8 Y:20 K:0
R:152 G:200 B:205

C:82 M:33 Y:54 K:0
R:11 G:134 B:126

Idea: Deliberately using old tones

The art of Ukiyo-e printmaking was prominently developed during the Edo period. Its bold colors, themes and designs attracted many people, both local and international. Even today, there are many people at home and abroad who seek out and collect Ukiyo-e works. They enjoy the charm of one of the most famous art forms in Japan and its unique woodcut printing technique. This set of works imitates the tones and schemes of Ukiyo-e works during the Edo period.

井上 探景画

13

Monmon Cats

Designer: Kazuaki Horitomo Kitamura

C:30 M:2 Y:10 K:0
R:188 G:224 B:231

C:50 M:4 Y:74 K:0
R:141 G:193 B:99

C:10 M:95 Y:100 K:0
R:217 G:40 B:23

C:0 M:0 Y:0 K:15
R:230 G:230 B:230

C:58 M:32 Y:15 K:0
R:118 G:154 B:188

C:20 M:82 Y:73 K:0
R:203 G:78 B:64

Idea: Colors correlate with local culture and things

Monmon Cats encompass a unique concept that combines 2 of Kazuaki Horitomo Kitamura's favorite things: cats and tattoos. Monmon is a Japanese word that can mean tattoo, so Monmon Cats perfectly describes the artist's tattooed cat art. These tattoo patterns are mainly images and symbols found in Japanese art, culture and religion, such as the large red koi fish that represents luck and wealth; the black dragon that represents experience and wisdom; the black snake that represents wisdom, prophesy and health; the bright red peony that represents wealth, elegance and prosperity; the skull that represents change, the cycle of life and respect for ancestors; and falling red maple leaves that represent the passage of time.

14

Poster Designs

Designer: Ryu Mieno

Idea: Comparison between schemes and formats

Ryu Mieno graduated from Kyoto Seika University in 2011 and is now a freelance designer. His designs involve a wide range of elements. He is a member of the mural art team "uwn!" and is now in charge of the design of "AT PAPER" in *FREE MAGAZINE*. These posters have an avant-garde format but possess a retro color scheme. This creates visual contrast within a single picture.

Aichi Prefectural Art Theater
16th AAF Drama Award
Commemorative Performance Poster
2017

C:59 M:0 Y:17 K:0
R:97 G:195 B:213

C:95 M:0 Y:82 K:0
R:0 G:158 B:95

C:0 M:36 Y:43 K:0
R:247 G:184 B:142

C:0 M:58 Y:48 K:0
R:240 G:137 B:114

The Kyoto Experiment International Performing Arts Festival Poster
2016

C:33 M:0 Y:18 K:0
R:181 G:222 B:217

C:0 M:0 Y:20 K:0
R:255 G:252 B:219

The Tsushima Art Festival Key Visual Poster
2017

小寺鳩甫と酒井七馬

〜『大阪パック』から「新寶島」まで〜

平成二十八年九月八日（木）〜十一月八日（火）

会場：京都国際マンガミュージアム

The Kyoto International Manga Museum Poster
2016

15

Posters for the 2012 World Table Tennis Championships

Studio: Dentsu
Designer: Yuri Uenish

Idea: Matching colors and lines

To show the "speed" and "momentum" of table tennis, the designer used the effect line (radial line) as the theme for the 2012 World Table Tennis Championships posters. This type of line is commonly seen in comics and cartoons. Normally, people tend to use a lot of color to attract attention, but her posters stand out by having only black and white ink on gold paper.

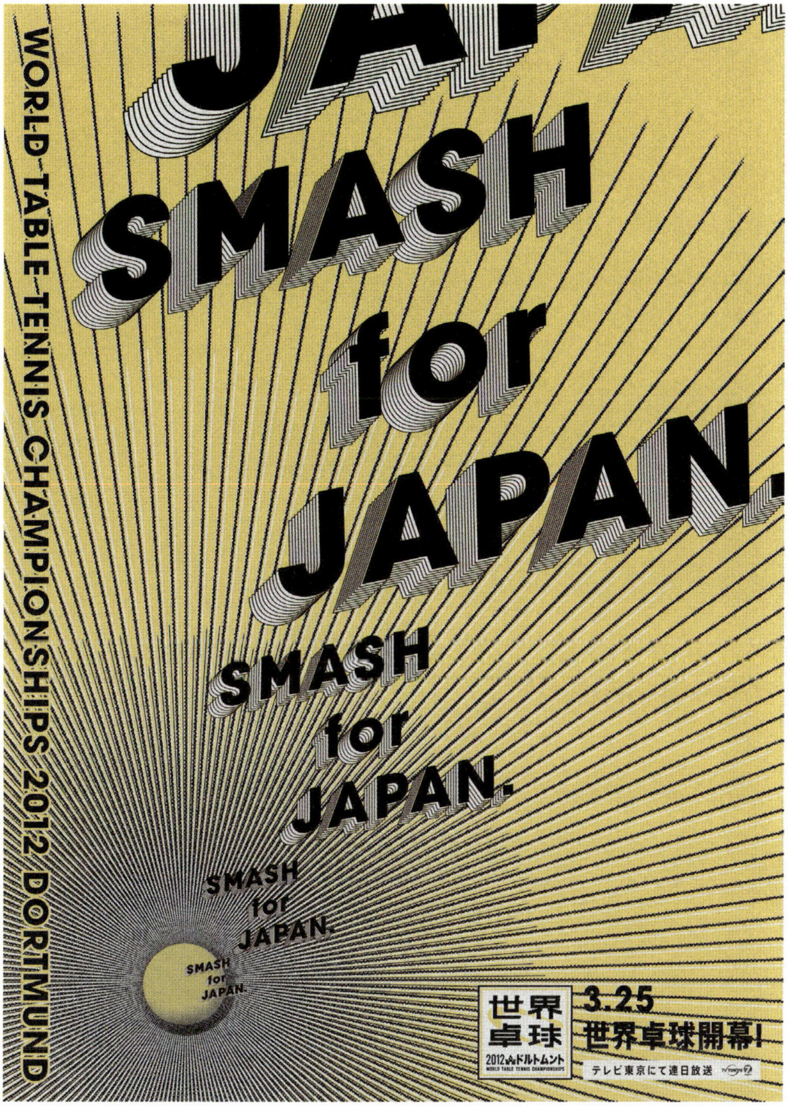

WORLD TABLE TENNIS CHAMPIONSHIPS 2012 DORTMUND

SMASH for JAPAN.

SMASH for JAPAN.

SMASH for JAPAN.

SMASH for JAPAN.

世界卓球 2012ドルトムント WORLD TABLE TENNIS CHAMPIONSHIPS

3.25 世界卓球開幕!

テレビ東京にて連日放送

16

Renovation

Designer: Hiroko Takahashi

Idea: A classic combination of black, white and gold

To celebrate the opening of his studio in Oshiage, Japan, designer Hiroko Takahashi held a kimono exhibition. The studio was once an old factory. To fit the atmosphere of the studio, she re-dyed a collection of old kimonos and integrated traditional Japanese embroidery patterns and woven details. The classic, timeless combination of black, white and gold transcends time and space, placing history before people's eyes.

17

U.I.J × Nimura Daisuke Project

Illustrator: Nimura Daisuke

U.I.J × Nimura daisuke

C:53 M:59 Y:75 K:6
R:136 G:108 B:75

C:89 M:65 Y:83 K:44
R:19 G:59 B:46

Idea: Achieve a sense of balance through color matching

At the invitation of U.I.J Hotel & Hostel, the illustrator Nimura Daisuke used his unique sense of humor to create 2 cute characters for the brand — "Hotel Girl" and "Hostel Boy". This co-branded project successfully delivers the spirit of U.I.J — "Reading and traveling are both important ways to explore the world and oneself". The playful and quirky characters are complemented by the dark brown and green color scheme, making the pictures balanced and playful.

U.I.J
2017
HOTEL & HOSTEL
× Nimura daisuke

NO FOOD
AFTER 10 PM
NO VISITORS

U.I.J 2017 HOTEL & HOSTEL × **Nimura daisuke**

18 Series of Posters

Designer: Kazumasa Nagai

JAPAN

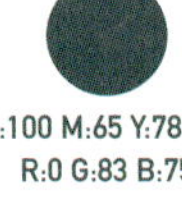

C:100 M:65 Y:78 K:9
R:0 G:83 B:75

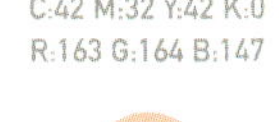

C:42 M:32 Y:42 K:0
R:163 G:164 B:147

C:2 M:27 Y:35 K:0
R:246 G:202 B:165

JAPAN 1998

C:100 M:55 Y:82 K:17
R:0 G:88 B:70

C:37 M:50 Y:96 K:0
R:177 G:134 B:38

C:0 M:0 Y:0 K:35
R:191 G:192 B:192

JAPAN 1998

Poster for Exhibition "World of Kazumasa Nagai"
1980

C:30 M:38 Y:89 K:0
R:192 G:159 B:50

C:0 M:0 Y:93 K:0
R:255 G:241 B:0

C:83 M:79 Y:5 K:3
R:66 G:67 B:147

C:0 M:91 Y:99 K:0
R:232 G:53 B:15

C:90 M:38 Y:93 K:18
R:0 G:108 B:60

C:98 M:88 Y:0 K:8
R:16 G:49 B:139

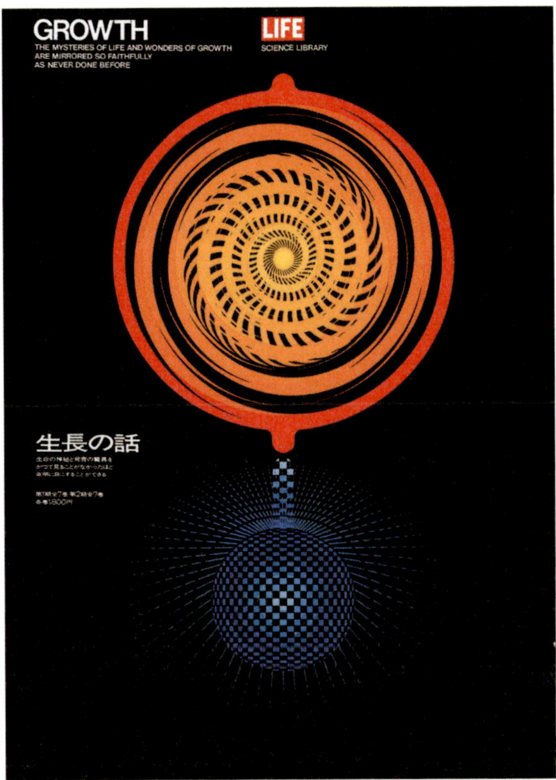

Life-Science Library The Story of Life 1966

Colors of Lilies 1974

C:0 M:97 Y:95 K:0
R:230 G:25 B:25

C:0 M:27 Y:97 K:0
R:251 G:196 B:0

C:99 M:75 Y:14 K:0
R:0 G:73 B:144

C:95 M:30 Y:9 K:0
R:0 G:131 B:194

C:53 M:65 Y:71 K:7
R:135 G:98 B:77

C:16 M:0 Y:81 K:0
R:227 G:229 B:68

Idea: Simple composition and color matching create a strong effect

Kazumasa Nagai is a master of Japanese graphic design and has won numerous JAGDA awards. His works combine classic Japanese aesthetics and elegant modern styles.

He uses a simple composition, minimal colors, and a pure interweaving of dots and lines to convey important thought-provoking ideas on life. Everything on his posters becomes vivid through interweaving dots and simple hand-drawn lines, allowing audiences to feel the pure pulse of nature. In his works, he uses traditional Japanese aesthetic elements such as Japanese floral patterns and color schemes. Based on this aesthetic, he further combines Zen philosophy and scientific design with his understanding of the mysteries of life.

19

Shoyeido

Idea: Cultural inheritance in storefront design

Shoyeido, a Japanese incense brand in Kyoto, was founded during the Edo period (1705) and has handed down its traditional art of handmade incense through 12 generations.

Unlike the time-honored shop, Lisn, a sub-brand of Shoyeido, adopts a new and modern style. According to the different themes released each year, Lisn collaborates with different types of artists, such as photographers, illustrators and embroidery artists, to explore and create new fragrances. For example, for the theme "cue", Lisn collaborated with illustrator Rodrigo Pareja to present products showing the changing seasons. In another case, bookbinding artist Akie Tsuzuki handcrafted special "present"-themed packaging for Lisn.

C:40 M:51 Y:0 K:0
R:166 G:134 B:188

C:10 M:13 Y:29 K:0
R:234 G:222 B:189

C:53 M:71 Y:56 K:0
R:141 G:92 B:97

C:43 M:45 Y:79 K:0
R:163 G:140 B:74

C:26 M:2 Y:28 K:0
R:200 G:225 B:198

C:41 M:38 Y:21 K:0
R:164 G:157 B:175

C:20 M:47 Y:36 K:0
R:208 G:152 B:144

C:18 M:22 Y:43 K:0
R:217 G:198 B:153

山里

In addition to their innovation in incense products, 2 Lisn stores designed by interior designer Shigemasa Noi, Lisn Kyoto and Lisn Aoyama, possess a simple, modern style that is different from the old Shoyeido store. Both Lisn stores are creative in visualizing the image of incense.

Inside the Lisn Kyoto store, the smooth curves of the plaster walls create a sense of flowing and lingering incense smoke. Similarly, the glass product display tables also utilize smooth curves, with slender copper bars interspersed like incense sticks. For the Lisn Aoyama store, its design concept lets in natural light to illuminate the whole space. The lighting fixtures in the store are wrapped in spiral-like washi paper and look like rising smoke. The slightest flicker creates changes in shadow and light.

Whether it is an old or new store, the timeless vitality and value of the 300-year-old Shoyeido incense brand can be seen in its different store designs. People can get a glimpse of its inheritance of Japan's ancient incense culture and its innovation to fit into modern life.

C:50 M:30 Y:79 K:0
R:146 G:158 B:81

C:0 M:42 Y:50 K:0
R:245 G:171 B:124

C:18 M:27 Y:58 K:0
R:217 G:188 B:119

C:13 M:33 Y:44 K:0
R:224 G:182 B:143

C:24 M:10 Y:11 K:0
R:203 G:217 B:222

C:90 M:70 Y:0 K:0
R:29 G:80 B:162

C:6 M:21 Y:90 K:0
R:242 G:204 B:22

C:24 M:88 Y:66 K:0
R:195 G:62 B:71

20

SOU·SOU

Designers: Katsuji Wakisaka, Hisanobu Tsujimura, Takeshi Wakabayashi

Idea: Japanese Kyoto style revealed through colors

SOU·SOU, a fabric brand that first appeared in Tokyo, manufactures and sells products characteristic of Japanese culture, including traditional split-toe work shoes (jikatabi), kimono, traditional cloth for wrapping (furoshiki) and hand towels (tenugui). The words "sou-sou", which mean "yes, quite so", are commonplace in daily Japanese communication and are reminiscent of 2 people expressing agreement. Based on this concept, the 3 co-founders of the brand express their respective understandings of traditional Japanese culture in an endeavor to draw people's attention to that culture. The theme of this series is on the changing of seasons, and it features natural elements such as flowers and trees in different seasons and seasonal fruits and vegetables. Naturally, red leaves, wagashi, the moon and other elements associated with Kyoto can be found in the series. The selected colors are strongly characteristic of Kyoto and maintain a traditional pattern that carries an authentic and tranquil Japanese flavor.

C:71 M:9 Y:75 K:0
R:67 G:168 B:100

C:38 M:5 Y:74 K:0
R:175 G:204 B:95

C:0 M:80 Y:51 K:0
R:234 G:84 B:92

C:80 M:50 Y:0 K:0
R:48 G:113 B:185

C:4 M:84 Y:58 K:0
R:227 G:73 B:80

C:70 M:16 Y:0 K:0
R:48 G:166 B:223

C:90 M:69 Y:0 K:0
R:26 G:81 B:163

C:71 M:66 Y:0 K:0
R:95 G:92 B:167

C:36 M:99 Y:77 K:0
R:174 G:32 B:57

C:89 M:54 Y:58 K:7
R:2 G:100 B:103

C:19 M:57 Y:7 K:0
R:207 G:133 B:174

C:44 M:21 Y:7 K:0
R:153 G:182 B:214

C:28 M:22 Y:0 K:0
R:192 G:194 B:226

C:51 M:45 Y:13 K:0
R:140 G:138 B:178

C:13 M:17 Y:69 K:0
R:229 G:207 B:98

C:2 M:60 Y:19 K:0
R:236 G:133 B:156

C:0 M:34 Y:4 K:0
R:246 G:192 B:211

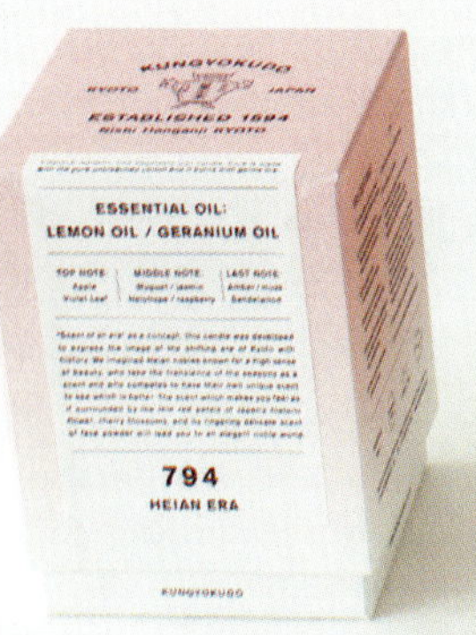

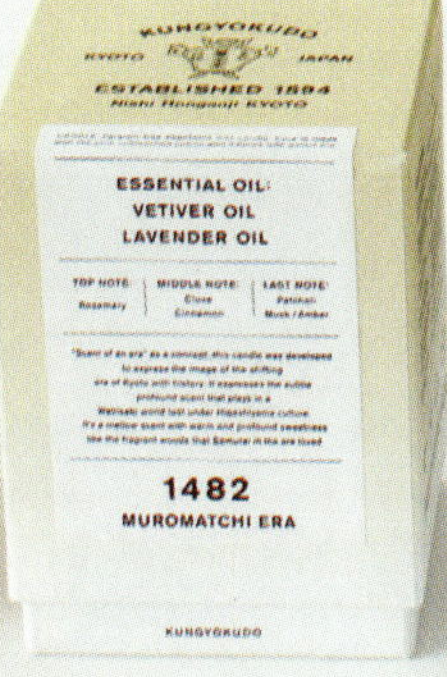

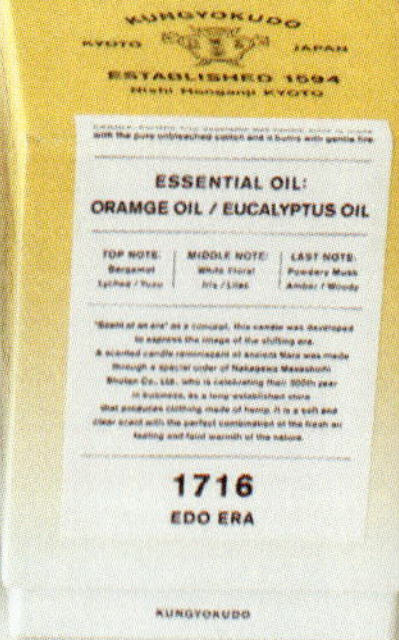

21

Kungyokudo

Studio: good design company
Creative Director: Manabu Mizuno

Idea: Monochrome colors that gradually change color

Founded in 1594, Kungyokudo boasts 428 years of history and time-honored traditions. The brand is committed to the production of unique incense for ceremonial occasions and daily life. Manufacturing recipes that include names for ingredients, such as old trees and herbs used in Chinese medicine, are passed down from generation to generation.

For the packaging of incense, candles and long matches, the studio chose a modern and elegant design that showcases Kungyokudo's innovativeness. The incense colors draw inspiration from local scenery, and the incense texture is almost identical to that of Japanese paper. The candles gradually change colors as they burn as if they are emitting fragrance into the air. Long matches and modern containers, which have broken away from traditional Japanese styles, have helped Kungyokudo build up its reputation both in Japan and overseas.

C:9 M:21 Y:8 K:0
R:233 G:211 B:218

C:9 M:9 Y:26 K:0
R:237 G:230 B:198

C:42 M:19 Y:7 K:0
R:158 G:187 B:216

C:8 M:17 Y:73 K:0
R:239 G:211 B:87

C:61 M:16 Y:100 K:0
R:113 G:167 B:46

C:88 M:57 Y:5 K:0
R:0 G:100 B:171

C:57 M:3 Y:14 K:0
R:105 G:194 B:217

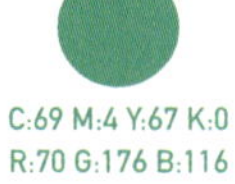
C:69 M:4 Y:67 K:0
R:70 G:176 B:116

C:4 M:83 Y:78 K:0
R:228 G:77 B:53

C:5 M:23 Y:86 K:0
R:244 G:201 B:43

C:33 M:3 Y:22 K:0
R:182 G:218 B:207

22

Musubi

Studio: Torafu Architects
Creative Directors: Koichi Suzuno, Shinya Kamuro
Photographer: Yousuke Tatsumi (healthy)

Idea: Achieve the best effects with the simplest colors

Musubi, a furoshiki manufacturer, participated in the Interior Lifestyle Design Expo. The design of its exhibition booth is shown here. The designer used white and wood-colored fixtures to form square frames to present the 3 furoshiki products Chomusubi, Cochae and Karacho on different walls. To demonstrate the many ways furoshiki can be used, the designer wrapped various items in colorful furoshiki and hung them in large square frames or from the ceiling, making them easy to see at a glance. The white and wood-colored installations not only set off the colorful products, but also provide visitors with a sense of neatness, brightness and simplicity.

むす
山田繊維株式会社

ちょうむすび
mina perhonen + musubi

23

Design of Tenugui

Studio: Watt
Designer: Mitsuko Ogura

C:94 M:89 Y:5 K:0
R:39 G:52 B:140

C:73 M:76 Y:16 K:0
R:94 G:77 B:141

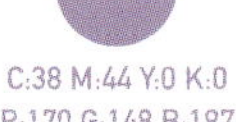

C:38 M:44 Y:0 K:0
R:170 G:148 B:197

C:59 M:20 Y:18 K:0
R:109 G:170 B:195

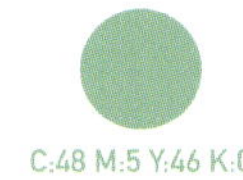

C:48 M:5 Y:46 K:0
R:144 G:197 B:157

C:0 M:37 Y:75 K:0
R:247 G:179 B:73

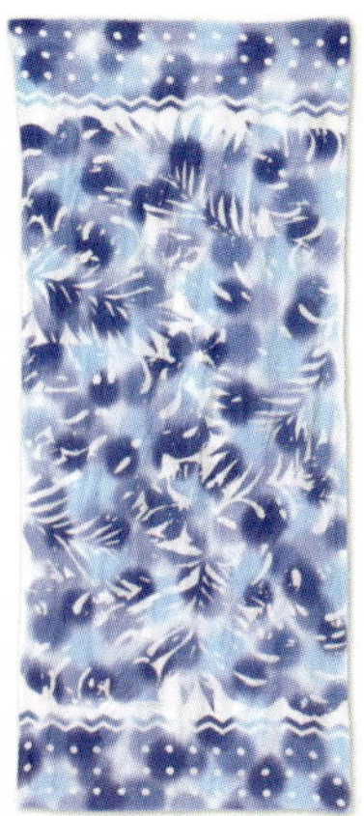

Idea: Integrating modern natural features with Edo period styles

In Japan, tenugui originally referred to head coverings that were used only by the rich and powerful when making offerings during religious ceremonies. Now, however, an increasing number of people use tenugui, which are rich in styles and colorful patterns. This series, co-designed by Mitsuko Ogura and the Watt Studio, applies the methods of printing and dyeing and has a distinctive style. The production process involves multiple steps including shaping, dyeing, tinting, painting, washing and drying. Ogura's design focuses on depicting humanistic features of the Edo Period and uses colors characteristic of that period. Watt Studio's design has a sense of modern civilization and tends to draw inspiration from nature, using colors that depict liveliness, youthfulness and energy.

C:86 M:57 Y:14 K:0
R:27 G:101 B:161

C:74 M:65 Y:55 K:12
R:83 G:87 B:96

C:52 M:74 Y:71 K:13
R:132 G:79 B:69

C:28 M:28 Y:38 K:0
R:195 G:181 B:158

C:72 M:69 Y:71 K:31
R:76 G:68 B:63

C:74 M:64 Y:54 K:0
R:89 G:96 B:106

C:47 M:40 Y:38 K:0
R:151 G:148 B:147

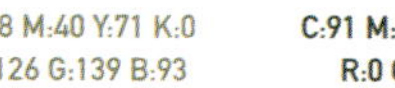

C:58 M:40 Y:71 K:0
R:126 G:139 B:93

C:91 M:50 Y:82 K:33
R:0 G:83 B:59

C:30 M:30 Y:39 K:0
R:190 G:176 B:154

ミニマリズム
Minimalism

Chapter

○ Matching a natural wood color with a solid color/ ○ Minimalist color gradient/ ○ Gradient colors formed through special printing/ ○ Fresh and natural/ ○ Simple, light colors create a fresh and advanced style/ ○ Blue & White — Fresh & Clean/ ○ Single color variation/ ○ Use a large dark blue area to express athletic tension/ ○ Aqua blue for the pureness of nature/ ○ Cool colors/ ○ Japanese New Year Red/ ○ Simple color balance/ ○ Using colors to highlight/ ○ Simple and bright color combination/ ○ Color block patterns/ ○ A single color for each category/ ○ Gradual dyeing/ ○ One color for each piece/ ○ Large single-color blocks/ ○ Use minimal colors to achieve ease and comfort/ ○ A simple and clear picture/ ○ Colorful graphics used in a large area/ ○ Gray and white background with monochrome blocks/ ○ Skillful choice of representative colors/ ○ Highlight the contrast between black and white with transparent color/ ○ Minimalist premium gold/ ○ Local representative colors/ ○ A large, single color block spreading over the picture/ ○ Leaving a large blank space/ ○ Use black and white to represent permanence

24

Lump-Bowl for Urushi Kobo Oshima

Studio: Kuroyanagi Jun Design Hut
Designer: nendo
Photographer: Akihiro Yoshida

Idea: Matching a natural wood color with a solid color

Nendo was invited to design a series of lacquer bowl products for Urushi Kobo Oshima, a traditional lacquerware workshop. Based on the workshop's mastery of wood scraping, nendo designed the lacquer bowl to evoke the user's awareness of woodworking by enlarging and rounding the base. This encourages the user to cradle the "lump" base in their hands naturally rather than grasping it. In turn, this creates a new experience of what it feels like to hold a bowl. The natural wood color and grain of the exterior contrasts softly with the solid-colored matte lacquer of the interior, showcasing the thickness of the wood and its unique texture.

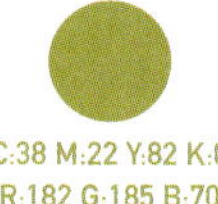

C:9 M:79 Y:15 K:0
R:220 G:84 B:138

C:65 M:0 Y:43 K:0
R:78 G:187 B:164

C:54 M:70 Y:4 K:0
R:137 G:92 B:160

C:17 M:9 Y:65 K:0
R:222 G:217 B:112

25

CMY/POT, CMY/YAMA

Studio: UMA/Design Farm
Designers: Yuma Harada, Yuka Tsuda
Photographer: Yoshiro Masuda
Manufacturer: Fukunaga Print Co., Ltd.

Idea: Minimalist color gradient

When CMY series products absorb water, the ink printed on the paper will change. The paper incorporates a mixture of cyan, magenta and yellow pigments that, due to gravity, create a beautiful color gradient when the paper absorbs water

26

TINT

Studio: UMA/Design Farm
Designer: Yuka Tsuda
Art Director: Yuma Harada
Photographer: Yoshiro Masuda

C:8 M:24 Y:31 K:0
R:236 G:203 B:175

C:16 M:14 Y:35 K:0
R:222 G:214 B:175

C:6 M:10 Y:8 K:0
R:242 G:233 B:231

C:8 M:36 Y:28 K:0
R:232 G:181 B:169

Idea: Gradient colors formed through special printing

TINT, made of synthetic paper, is a vase for a single dried flower. When illuminated, the 2 colors printed on the inner surface are reflected and blend together to create a gradation of colors on the outer surface. When placed on a brightly lit windowsill, the color is even more striking. The gradation changes depending on the environment and the weather.

27

Yuki Sawaya

Studio: 6D
Designers: Shogo Kishino, Miho Sakaki
Art Director: Shogo Kishino
Photographers: Shingo Fujimoto, Motonori Koga

Idea: Fresh and natural

Yuki-tsumugi is a unique Japanese silk-weaving technique with a history of over 2,000 years. It is an advanced technique done by hand and is listed as an Intangible Cultural Heritage by the United Nations. Kimonos made with this technique are soft, light and comfortable. With this in mind, the designer created a brand logo that depicts a hand and a long line. The hand represents the hand of the silk-weaver, while the line represents the silk thread used for weaving and also symbolizes the long history of the craft. Colors like emerald, light green and bright orange are used to convey feelings of workmanship, nature and credibility.

EYUKOM
Made in Japan
コメユ
米油
コメユ

Made in Japan
コメユ
米油
コメユ
KOMEYU
NET 110g
栄養機能食品

EYUKO
KOMEYU
in Japan
コメユ
米油
コメユ

KOMEYU
Made in Japan

28

Rice Bran Oil

Studio: Aromata, LLC
Designer: Shunsuke Aoki

Idea: Simple, light colors create a fresh and advanced style

The designer created this packaging for rice oil (also known as rice bran oil or RBO) with the intention of promoting the product to younger consumers. The designer used a soft and clean look to portray a sense of pure white that would allow it to fit into the environment of the store and have its place on the shelf among other products.

C:62 M:11 Y:16 K:0
R:92 G:179 B:206

C:10 M:69 Y:30 K:0
R:221 G:109 B:131

29

Koshi No Kanbai

Studio: Nippon Design Center
Designer: Daigo Daikoku

C:39 M:100 Y:99 K:5
R:164 G:31 B:37

一輪一滴
百十周年祝酒

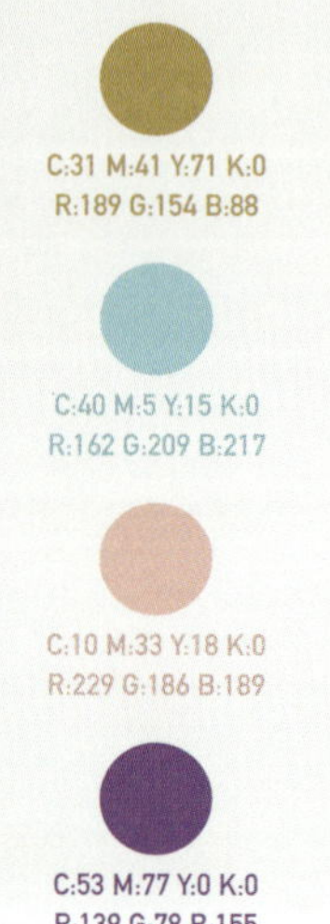
C:31 M:41 Y:71 K:0
R:189 G:154 B:88
C:40 M:5 Y:15 K:0
R:162 G:209 B:217
C:10 M:33 Y:18 K:0
R:229 G:186 B:189
C:53 M:77 Y:0 K:0
R:139 G:78 B:155

越乃寒梅
特醸酒
自家製焼酎仕込
KOSHI NO KANBAI
日本酒
720ml

越乃寒梅
灑
純米吟醸
KOSHI NO KANBAI
日本酒
720ml

越乃寒梅
無垢
純米大吟醸
KOSHI NO KANBAI
日本酒
720ml

越乃寒梅
特撰
吟醸
KOSHI NO KANBAI
日本酒
720ml

越乃寒梅
醇良
石本酒造株式会社
ISHIMOTO SAKE BREWERY

越乃寒梅
山田錦
特醸酒
石本酒造株式会社
ISHIMOTO SAKE BREWERY

Idea: Blue & White — Fresh & Clean

This premium sake was promoted to commemorate the 110th anniversary of Ishimoto Sake Brewery. The logo includes a hexagonal snowflake and a ring of plum blossoms. The font was adapted from an existing typeface to depict the fresh and clean flavor of sake. The pattern originates from "a village sandwiched between 2 rivers". To reflect Juzo Ishimoto's philosophy of "bold and delicate", the designer used foil stamping and embossing to inject a core sense of calmness and quiet beauty into the seemingly blank design.

C:93 M:67 Y:0 K:0
R:0 G:83 B:165

C:45 M:0 Y:12 K:0
R:146 G:210 B:225

"Sai" is Ishimoto Sake Brewery's first new brand in 40 years. The vibrant blue bottle and light brown label represent the soft and smooth flavor of the sake. The designer also created newspaper ads and brochures for promotional sales.

30

Echigo Tsurukame Seasonal Limited Edition

Studio: Kuroyanagi Jun Design Hut
Designer: Kuroyanagi Jun

C:50 M:0 Y:99 K:0
R:143 G:195 B:34

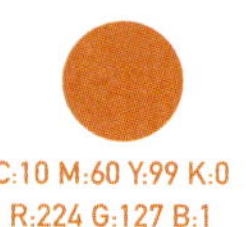

C:10 M:60 Y:99 K:0
R:224 G:127 B:1

C:79 M:35 Y:87 K:0
R:53 G:132 B:75

C:18 M:0 Y:47 K:0
R:220 G:232 B:159

Idea: Single color variation

This is the bottle design for Japanese sake brand Echigo Tsurukame's seasonal limited edition. The center pattern is inspired by the "crane" and "turtle", 2 symbols of auspiciousness and longevity common in Japanese culture. For this product series, the motif pattern remains the same while the colors of the bottle and cap vary according to the season. The flavor of Japanese sake changes with the seasons during the brewing and maturation processes, and each season has its own unique flavor. For example, a change in the packaging from salmon pink to caramel reflects a change in the flavor. The whole idea of the design is to show the richness of life brought by the changing seasons.

WORLD TABLE TENNIS
CHAMPIONSHIPS 2015

31

Posters for the 2015 World Table Tennis Championships

Studios: Dentsu, J.C. Spark
Designers: Yuri Uenish, Toshinori Obuchi
Creative Director: Mari Konishi
Photographer: Mikiya Takimoto

Idea: Use a large dark blue area to express athletic tension

The theme for the 2015 World Table Tennis Championships posters is "The Moment". The designer tried to freeze the moment with players being "as fast as still" to express the tension during the crucial moment of the game. The large dark blue background was designed to show the focus in table tennis as well as the tenacity and athletic tension of the players in a dramatic way.

C:91 M:65 Y:9 K:0
R:2 G:88 B:159

C:49 M:24 Y:19 K:0
R:142 G:173 B:191

32

Kirin Natural Mineral Water

Studio: SAGA Inc.
Designer: Kota Sagae
Creative Director: Tatsuya Hamajima

C:100 M:79 Y:8 K:0
R:0 G:66 B:146

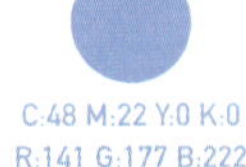

C:48 M:22 Y:0 K:0
R:141 G:177 B:222

C:78 M:15 Y:11 K:0
R:0 G:160 B:207

Idea: Aqua blue for the pureness of nature

This is the packaging designed by SAGA Inc. for Kirin Natural Mineral Water. Water bottles have become a part of the interior. Realizing this, the designer tries to design packaging that can blend well with the living space. Kirin bottles lack advertising slogans that are prominent on other "wordy" designs. To deliver the brand's philosophy of "water and nature", the designer used aqua blue and soft blue, as well as water drops, trees and other natural patterns to enhance the quiet and relaxing feeling of nature.

KIRIN
キリンのやわらか天然水
NATURAL MINERAL WATER
2L

KIRIN
キリンのやわらか天然水
NATURAL MINERAL WATER
2L
ケース商品コード
ITFコード

33

2D/3D Chairs

Designer: Yoichi Yamamoto

Idea: Cool colors

Yoichi Yamamoto designed this installation for Issey Miyake's flagship store to express its philosophy of going "from 2D cloth to 3D dress". If you look at the hats from a certain point of view in front of the shop window, the design presents an illusion as if the hat were resting upon a "chair". In fact, it is only a single figure merged and created by a 3-dimensional back and 2-dimensional legs. The color of the "chair" was decided by the client, who, with a keen sense of color, chose a cool navy blue, bringing coolness and pleasant feelings to customers during the hotter months.

34

Pocchiri

Studio: Draft Co., Ltd.
Designer: Eriko Kawakami
Creative Director: Ryusuke Tanaka

Idea: Japanese New Year Red

These small bags are produced by a long-established in Kyoto. Designed with the theme of "Happy Japanese New Year", its logo, graphics and main color are all red, the symbolic color of the Japanese New Year.

C:9 M:92 Y:76 K:0
R:219 G:50 B:54

pocchiri
made in japan
since 2012

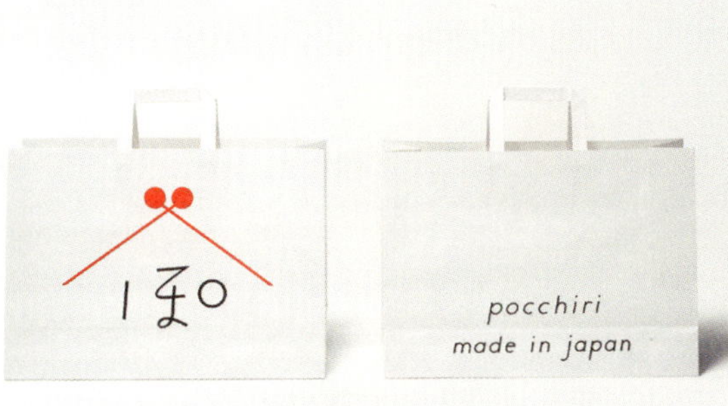
pocchiri
made in japan

35

A Halloween Poster for Aoyama Flower Market

Studio: Draft Co., Ltd.
Designer: Hiroka Osada
Art Director: Eriko Kawakami

C:2 M:69 Y:89 K:0
R:235 G:111 B:35

Idea: Simple color balance

This is the poster designed for the Aoyama Flower Market Halloween event. Since the poster would be surrounded by flowers of different colors, the designer decided to minimize the color on the poster to achieve balance. Grotesque illustrations and gray and black are used to present the Halloween theme, with bright orange pumpkins further conveying the colors of the season.

36

365'19 Calendar

Studio: KIGI Co., Ltd.
Designer: Mayu Morimoto
Art Director: Ryosuke Uehara

Idea: Using colors to highlight

This large calendar makes bold use of the traditional Swiss font Helvetica. Following the concept of "every day can be someone's important day", the designer ensures that all of the important days are given enough attention by using different colored numbers, circles and slashes.

C:80 M:22 Y:62 K:0
R:1 G:154 B:123

C:17 M:11 Y:90 K:0
R:233 G:220 B:1

C:96 M:90 Y:0 K:0
R:31 G:49 B:143

37

Bubu

Studio: Draft Co., Ltd.
Designer: Eriko Kawakami
Creative Director: Ryusuke Tanaka

C:29 M:33 Y:75 K:0
R:194 G:169 B:82

C:46 M:18 Y:53 K:0
R:153 G:181 B:136

C:13 M:55 Y:27 K:0
R:219 G:139 B:150

C:80 M:73 Y:32 K:0
R:74 G:81 B:127

Idea: Simple and bright color combination

Bubu is a Japanese grocery store for families. Many of its products are aimed at children, so the designer chose bright colors with a Japanese style and triangle graphics.

C:2 M:41 Y:0 K:0
R:241 G:177 B:206

C:0 M:97 Y:96 K:0
R:230 G:25 B:23

C:11 M:19 Y:26 K:0
R:231 G:211 B:189

C:87 M:55 Y:4 K:0
R:3 G:103 B:175

C:92 M:57 Y:100 K:34
R:0 G:75 B:41

C:44 M:84 Y:100 K:12
R:149 G:65 B:34

38

D-BROS, New Year's Cards

Studio: Draft Co., Ltd.
Designer: Eriko Kawakami
Creative Director: Satoru Miyata

Idea: Color block patterns

D-BROS is a series of New Year's cards designed by the company Draft. To express the idea of fun, the designer used only a few brightly colored blocks to depict patterns of funny animals, plants and scenery.

あん丸
静岡 / 菊川

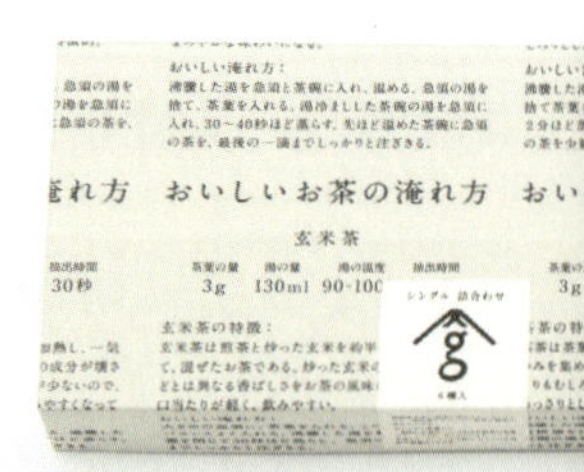
おいしい淹れ方：
おいしいお茶の淹れ方
玄米茶
3g 130ml
30秒

薄はり氷
静岡 / 菊川

39

Brand Promotion of San Grams, a Shop at Marumatsu Tea

Studio: Draft Co., Ltd.
Designer: Asako Koyama
Creative Director: Satoru Miyata
Photographer: Kenshu Shintsubo

Idea: A single color for each category

Marumatsu Tea Corporation is a century-old tea shop in Shizuoka Prefecture, Japan. With the increase of PET bottle use, sales of tea leaves that need to be brewed in tea pots declined. As a result, Marumatsu asked the designer to create a new brand design to convey its longing to raise the value of tea and the industry.

The designer decided to focus on the "character" of the tea leaves produced by Marumatsu. Based on the idea of wanting to offer delicious tea to people, San Grams (a place to taste tea) was opened. "San Grams" means "3 grams" ("san" is the Japanese pronunciation for "3"). This is because whether it is for deep-steamed green tea (fukamushicha), stem tea (kukicha), covered tea (kabusecha), roasted tea (hojicha), black tea, or oolong tea, the optimal amount of tea leaves to brew is 3 grams. The brand uses different colored packaging for the different types of tea, so that consumers can select their favorite at a glance. The producer's name and trade name, the tea's origin, flavor and regional characteristics are labeled on the package, and the brewing method is printed on the outer box to visually convey the deliciousness of the tea.

C:0 M:55 Y:0 K:0
R:239 G:147 B:187

C:55 M:0 Y:50 K:0
R:120 G:196 B:151

C:80 M:57 Y:63 K:9
R:62 G:98 B:93

40

Fukunaga Print

Studio: UMA/Design Farm
Designer: Yuka Tsuda
Art Director: Yuma Harada

Idea: Gradual dyeing

This is the New Year's greeting card from Fukunaga Print Co., Ltd. In traditional Japanese culture, if one dreams of "Mount Fuji, an eagle or an eggplant" at the beginning of the New Year, then it is a lucky sign. The artwork is printed with water-based pigments, so the melting ice can help spread the colors and dye the card.

C:16 M:54 Y:0 K:0
R:212 G:140 B:186

C:80 M:15 Y:28 K:0
R:0 G:158 B:180

C:77 M:72 Y:42 K:4
R:81 G:81 B:113

C:32 M:44 Y:67 K:0
R:186 G:149 B:94

41

Chocolate-Paint

Studio: nendo
Designer: Oki Sato
Photographer: Ayao Yamazaki

C:65 M:76 Y:76 K:40
R:82 G:54 B:48

Idea: One color for each piece

This chocolate packaging looks like a set of watercolor paints. Each "paint box" has a variety of colors, representing different flavors of chocolate. This design combines our childhood excitement of opening a new box of paints with the pleasure of opening a box of chocolates, providing those who open the box with a feeling of surprise.

42

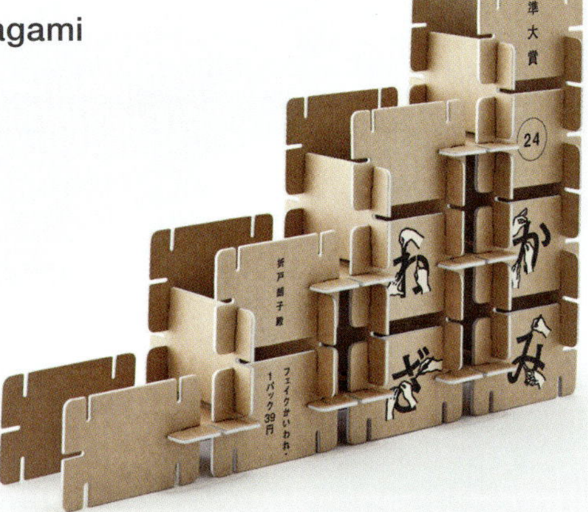

Paper Art Award

Studio: 6D
Designers: Shogo Kishino, Nozomi Tagami
Art Director: Shogo Kishino
Photographer: Shingo Fujimoto

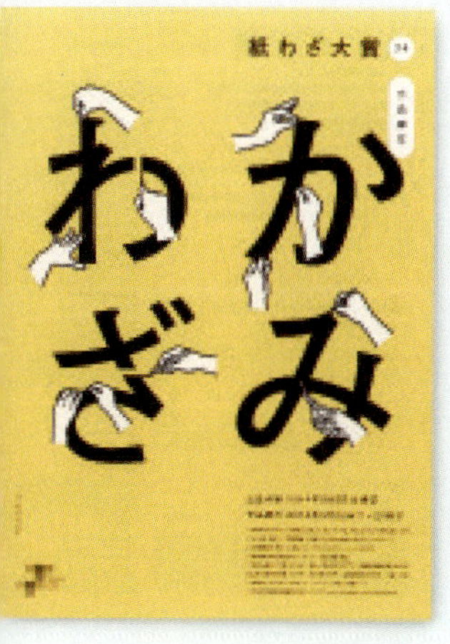

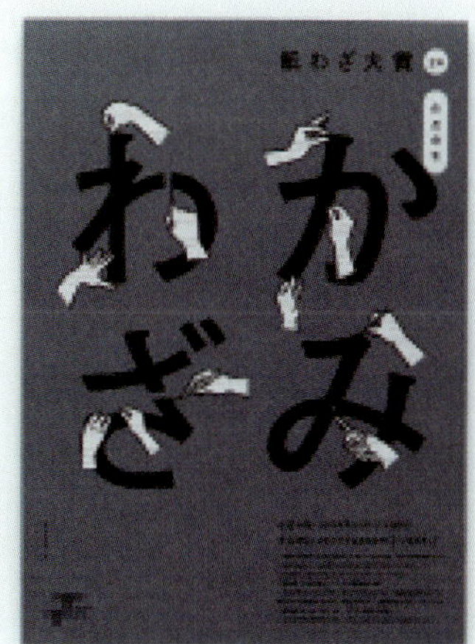

Idea: Large single-color blocks

This design was created for a paper art award. Since many of the participants enjoy creating things with paper, the design studio designed a logo to express the concept of "paper processing" and used it as the main visual element for posters and flyers. They also created a card-shaped trophy, the shape of which could be freely changed. Only one bright color was used for each trophy. They also designed an award certificate using a damascening inlay technique.

C:18 M:31 Y:43 K:0
R:215 G:183 B:146

C:0 M:0 Y:0 K:100
R:0 G:0 B:0

43

MUJI

Idea: Use minimal colors to achieve ease and comfort

Founded in 1980, MUJI has eliminated the unnecessary and created life's daily necessities. It adheres to the principles of "selecting materials", "modifying processes" and "simplifying packaging". These 3 principles are also reflected in all aspects of store décor and overall brand design. Whether its products, packaging or the store image, MUJI uses large blocks of natural wood color and white. This simple color scheme conveys the brand's philosophy of happiness, comfort, beauty, simplicity and rationality, allowing customers to discover the elegant and simple beauty of life.

44

Ise Ebiya

Studio: 6D-K
Designers: Shogo Kishino, Miho Sakai
Art Director: Shogo Kishino
Photographer: Shingo Fujimoto

Idea: A simple and clear picture

By creating the brand's logo in a traditional Japanese approach, it can be used well into the future. This represents the renewal of Ebiya's identity and visual design. Ebiya is a souvenir store located to the right of Ise Jingu Shrine and has a history of over 100 years. The design includes various symbols of Ise City and Ise Jingu, such as Ebisu, the god of wealth, and Japanese lobster, a local specialty. These symbols are the origin of the store's name and express the importance of the store as a representative of Ise in a land with a deep souvenir culture. Various elements are applied in different ways so that visitors can feel that they have taken a small piece of Ise home with them. Each logo uses only simple lines and no more than 2 colors to present a simple and clear picture.

C:4 M:71 Y:54 K:0
R:230 G:106 B:95

C:6 M:30 Y:24 K:0
R:237 G:194 B:182

C:24 M:30 Y:43 K:0
R:203 G:180 B:147

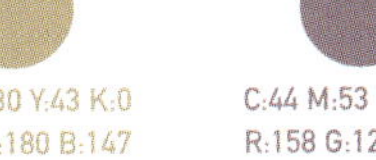

C:44 M:53 Y:24 K:0
R:158 G:128 B:155

C:80 M:58 Y:78 K:23
R:57 G:86 B:66

C:29 M:0 Y:11 K:0
R:191 G:227 B:231

C:24 M:22 Y:87 K:0
R:206 G:189 B:53

C:79 M:58 Y:71 K:15
R:64 G:92 B:79

C:67 M:0 Y:29 K:0
R:61 G:186 B:190

C:52 M:15 Y:5 K:0
R:127 G:184 B:222

C:16 M:32 Y:36 K:0
R:219 G:183 B:158

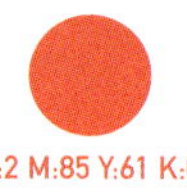

C:2 M:85 Y:61 K:0
R:230 G:71 B:76

45

JINS Abano Walk Store

Studio: KIGI Co., Ltd.
Designer: Mei Otsubo
Art Directors: Ryosuke Uehara, Yoshie Watanabe

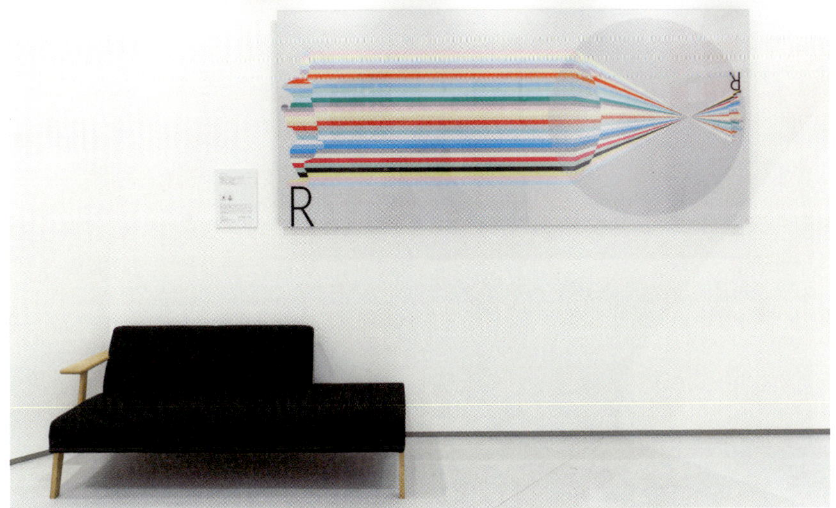

Idea: Colorful graphics used in a large area

Established in 2012 by Ryosuke Uehara and Yoshie Watanabe, the 2 artistic directors of the design company Draft's own label D-BROS, KIGI is dedicated to putting their unique ideas and boundless creativity into a broad series of different expressions that often intertwine with each other.

Through the interior decoration of JINS Abano Walk, designers aim to "send a message" through the product graphics and make a breakthrough. Colorful graphic signs made through KIGI filters add color to the shop with massive pictures stretching from floor to ceiling to inspire a better shopping experience.

46

Dear Mayuko

Studio: Nippon Design Center
Designer: Daigo Daikoku

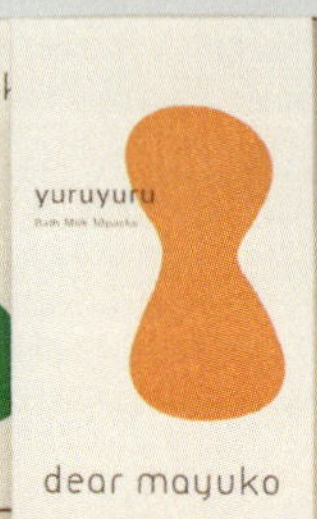

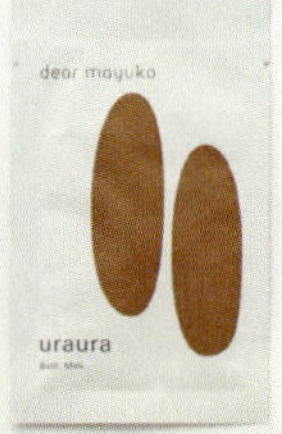

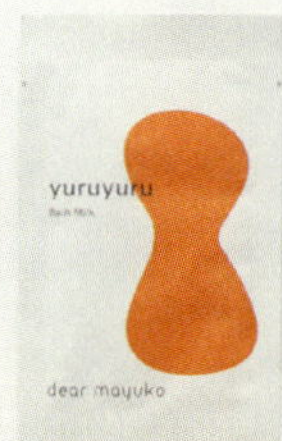

Idea: Gray and white background with monochrome blocks

Dear Mayuko is a lifestyle brand focusing on skincare and cosmetics. Its main ingredient is ozokerite — a natural cosmetic ingredient found in silk cocoons. The logo incorporates circular color blocks resembling cocoons to convey a plush, silky, shiny feeling when using the brand's shampoos and facial cleansing products. The brand's characteristic oval monochrome blocks are mainly used on labels, logos and packaging.

Promotional items such as shopping bags, gift boxes and catalogues adopt a 125mm×125mm grid pattern, which is in line with the specifications and appearance of the interior walls of the shop. These grid patterns form a sharp contrast to the circular color blocks on the package.

dear mayuko
dear mayuko
dear mayuko
dear mayuko

dear mayuko

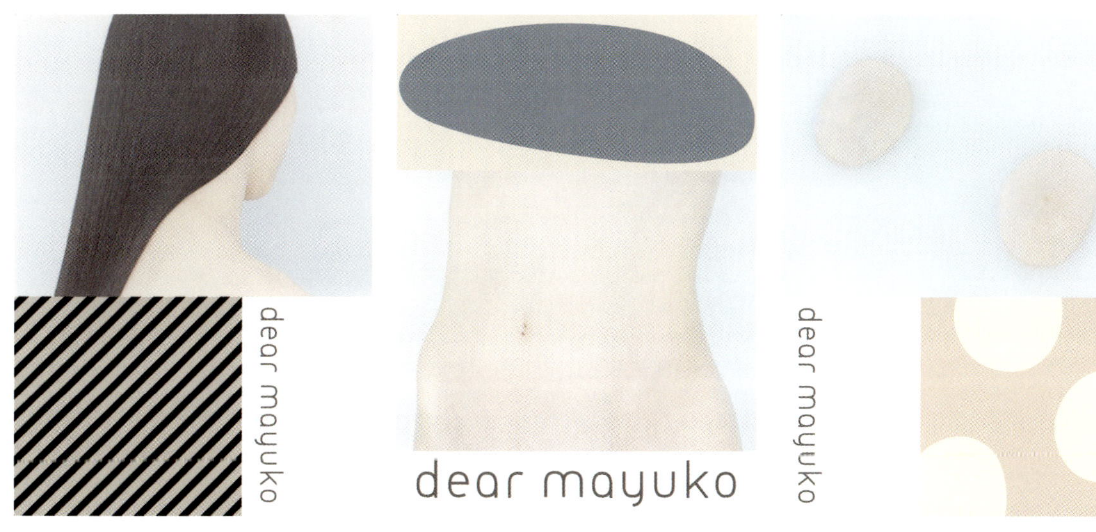
dear mayuko
dear mayuko
dear mayuko

47

1 Week Salad

Studio: nendo
Designer: Oki Sato
Photographer: Akihiro Yoshida

C:65 M:10 Y:60 K:0
R:91 G:174 B:127

C:39 M:17 Y:67 K:0
R:177 G:192 B:107

C:10 M:10 Y:60 K:0
R:237 G:222 B:123

C:10 M:64 Y:58 K:0
R:222 G:120 B:94

C:65 M:23 Y:13 K:0
R:90 G:169 B:210

C:58 M:59 Y:12 K:0
R:130 G:115 B:172

C:0 M:60 Y:5 K:0
R:238 G:134 B:174

Idea: Skillful choice of representative colors

1 Week Salad is an organic vegetable salad launched by nendo. To demonstrate the naturalness and freshness of the vegetables, completely transparent packaging cups are used so consumers can see the green vegetables inside. Each cup is also topped with a colorful piece of paper, with each color representing a salad dressing. The colorful wrapping paper contrasts with the transparent cups to provide a pleasant, varied and healthy experience for consumers.

03
Dark chocolate / Rhubarb / Violet.
¥1,300
08
09
Milk chocolate / Passion fruit.
¥1,300
05
Dark chocolate / Cherries / Lemon.
¥1,300
07
Dark chocolate / Raspberry.
¥1,300
23
14

48

BbyB

Studio: nendo
Photographer: Daici Ano

Idea: Highlight the contrast between black and white with transparent color

BbyB is a chocolate shop that offers 30 unique flavors of chocolate, including strawberry, pepper, lemon, passion fruit and basil. As all the chocolates are packaged in a modular manner with an almost identical design, it is difficult for customers to distinguish the different flavors of chocolate merely by their shape. Therefore, the designer began by choosing a unique packaging color for each distinctive flavor of chocolate. In addition, in order to highlight the different packaging colors, the display cases in the shop are completely see-through, with the chocolate inside appearing to float.

As for the interior design, the shop is all white in the front and all black in the café at the back of the shop. The contrast between black and white is even starker against the transparent display cases.

C:10 M:52 Y:68 K:0
R:226 G:145 B:84

C:59 M:0 Y:25 K:0
R:99 G:194 B:199

C:5 M:55 Y:29 K:0
R:232 G:143 B:147

C:10 M:13 Y:82 K:0
R:237 G:215 B:61

C:68 M:59 Y:0 K:0
R:100 G:105 B:175

C:54 M:15 Y:0 K:0
R:119 G:182 B:228

C:50 M:60 Y:65 K:0
R:147 G:112 B:91

15
25
35
41
19
27
36
42
23
28
38
48

49

Tabar

Studio: Draft Co., Ltd.
Designer: Eriko Kawakami
Photographer: Yasutomo Ebisu

Idea: Minimalist premium gold

Tabar is a brand that produces original tableware and metal products for business use. The designer used the "T" in Tabar as a table and combined it with lines and circles to form the logo. The product adopts the natural color of metal, which is coupled with a simple design to conjure a sense of luxury.

C:29 M:35 Y:62 K:0
R:193 G:167 B:108

C:100 M:95 Y:12 K:0
R:24 G:43 B:130

50

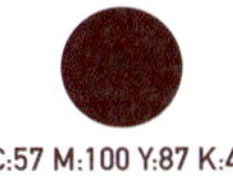
C:57 M:100 Y:87 K:49
R:87 G:0 B:24

C:10 M:20 Y:20 K:0
R:232 G:211 B:199

C:47 M:81 Y:100 K:14
R:146 G:69 B:21

Teavenir

Studio: Draft Co., Ltd.
Designer: Eriko Kawakami
Creative Director:
Ryusuke Tanaka

Idea: Local representative colors

This is an afternoon tea restaurant located in Kyoto, whose name Teavenir is a combination of Tea and Souvenir. This restaurant aims to provide visitors with the opportunity to honor their special memories in Kyoto with a leisurely afternoon tea. Taking full advantage of the old machiya (townhouses) elements, the designer has created a brand image that rebuilds the peaceful atmosphere of Kyoto. The designer also selected the representative color of the city, reddish brown, as the brand color.

51

Where Design Is Found

Studio: AYOND
Designer: Shun Sasaki

Idea: A large, single color block spreading over the picture

This is a dynamic poster designed for an exhibition of works that explores the history of modern design, with the shapes and colors changing according to different media.

デザインの
（居）場所

2019.5.21［火］
→ 6.30［日］
10:00–17:00（入館は16:30まで）
休館日：月曜日

国境／領域／時間

所蔵作品展

Where
design
is
found

東京国立近代美術館工芸館
Crafts Gallery,
The National Museum
of Modern Art,
Tokyo

MOMAT

C:0 M:86 Y:94 K:0
R:255 G:64 B:0

東京国立近代美術館工芸館
東京国立近代美術館工芸館
Crafts Gallery, The National Museum of Modern Art, Tokyo
所蔵作品展
MOMAT
Where design is found
国境／領域／時間
2019.5.21[火]
→ 6.30[日]
10:00–17:00 (入館は16:30まで)
休館日：月曜日
無料観覧日 6.2[日]
Free Admission Day: June 2 (Sun)
デザインの(居)場所

Crafts Gallery,
The National Museum
of Modern Art,
Tokyo

東京国立近代美術館工芸館

2019.5.21［火］
→ 6.30［日］
10:00–17:00（入館は16:30まで）
休館日：月曜日

MOMAT

所蔵作品展

国境／領域／時間

Where
design
is
found

デザインの
（居）場所

主催：東京国立近代美術館

C:68 M:0 Y:100 K:0
R:79 G:178 B:51

52

BEIGE Concept Store

Studio: nendo
Photographer: Takumi Ota

Idea: Leaving a large blank space

Fashion brand BEIGE has opened a new concept store in Takashimaya Shopping Mall in Tamagawa, a suburb of Tokyo. In addition to selling clothing and interior decorations, the store will also regularly hold activities such as book lending and art exhibitions. The designer divided the whole store into small spaces so that specific areas serve different functions. In order to avoid confusion, the whole concept store is mainly white with a wood color accent. Transparent glass is used to divide the space to maintain visual flexibility and cleanliness.

C:0 M:0 Y:0 K:0
R:255 G:255 B:255

BEIGE,

53

THINK OF THINGS

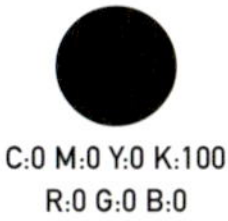

Idea: Use black and white to represent permanence

Opened by KOKUYO in Sendagaya, Tokyo, THINK OF THINGS is a lifestyle collection store. The first floor is a mixed area for cafes and products, the second floor is a multifunctional studio that can be rented, and the third is KOKUYO's internal work area. KOKUYO hopes to make various exchanges with customers and locals through this location and promote the research and development of products.

Although the shop is close to the bustling Harajuku and Omotesando neighborhoods, the owner hopes to maintain a leisurely and tranquil atmosphere in the store. The design of the store and products use black, white and wood colors to create a permanent, simple environment where customers can think and reflect on things in life.

かわいらしさ
Kawaii

Chapter

3

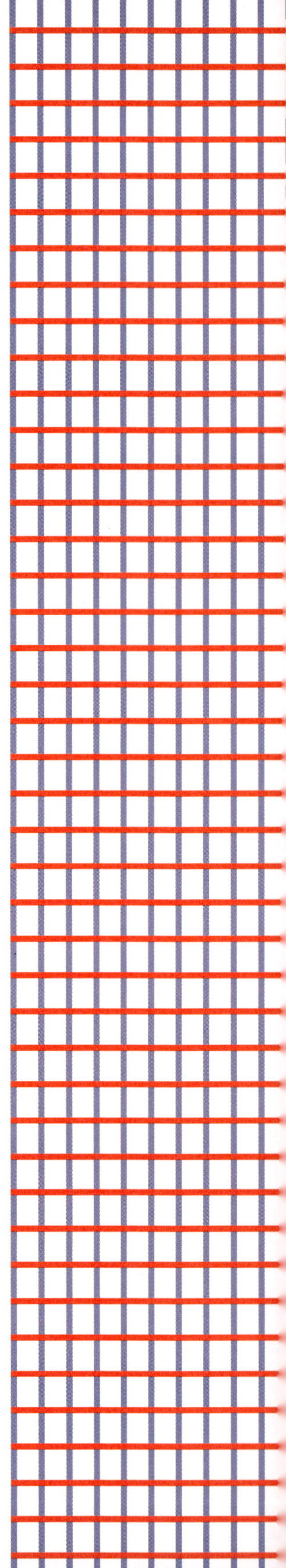

○ Large blocks of bright colors/ ○ Mix and match colors for adding interest/ ○ Fluorescent lines for a stronger visual effect/ ○ A colorful nature scene/ ○ Match colors with local features/ ○ Consistency in colors for a whole set/ ○ Use illustrations and color matching to create an overall lovely tone/ ○ Combining monochromes to create a sense of playfulness/ ○ Creating warmth from colors/ ○ Cute pink hue/ ○ A simple background color embellished with bright colors/ ○ Use light tones to reduce the sense of seriousness/ ○ Gentle color combinations with cartoon animals/ ○ Match colors and flavors/ ○ Colors that represent natural delight/ ○ A non-conventional choice of colors/ ○ Express emotions through colors/ ○ Colors create endless possibilities/ ○ Contrasting gold with bright colors/ ○ Strong color palettes create a positive atmosphere

54

Think Universal

Studio: Dentsu
Designers: Aya Yagi, Riko Ishizaki, Kumiko Shiraki, Ruriko Kasai
Art Director: Aya Yagi
Creative Director: Koji Kagoshima

C:2 M:30 Y:0 K:0
R:244 G:200 B:221

C:89 M:16 Y:0 K:0
R:0 G:151 B:220

C:69 M:0 Y:49 K:0
R:59 G:182 B:153

C:0 M:23 Y:68 K:0
R:252 G:206 B:96

C:0 M:85 Y:69 K:0
R:233 G:71 B:64

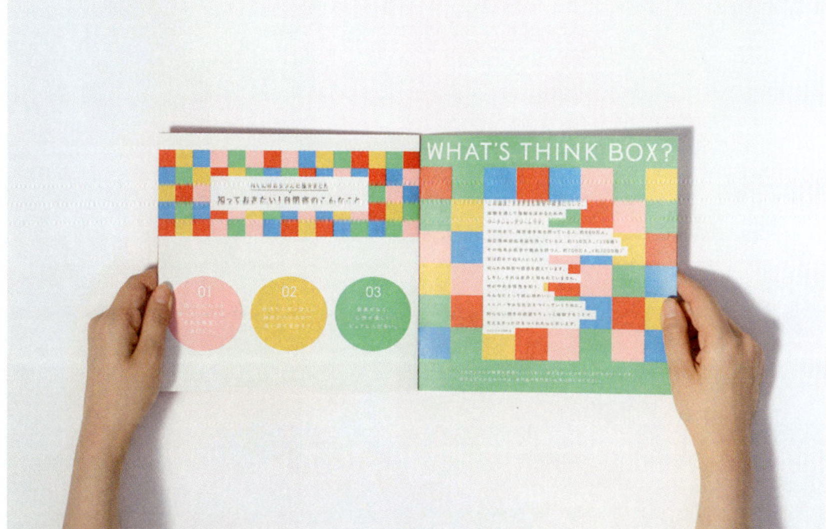

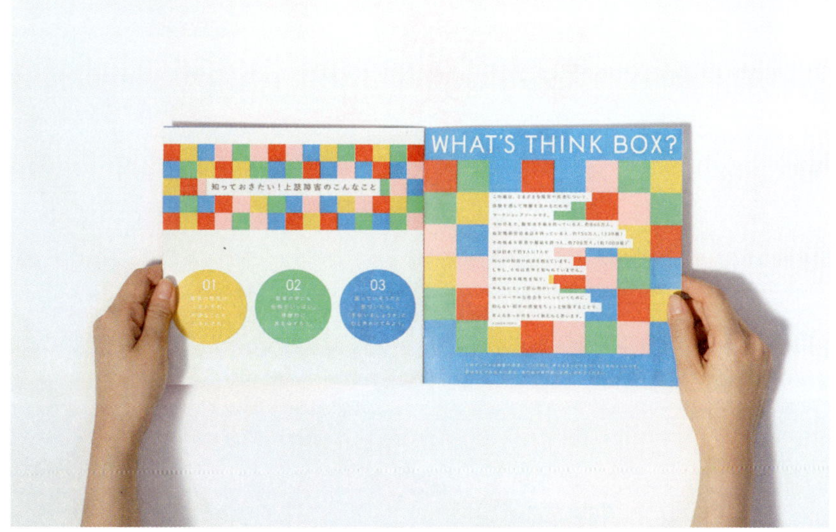

C:6 M:98 Y:86 K:0
R:222 G:22 B:40

C:72 M:0 Y:55 K:0
R:39 G:178 B:141

C:6 M:22 Y:75 K:0
R:242 G:203 B:79

Idea: Large blocks of bright colors

In Japan, one in nine people has some degree of disability or illness. However, the lives of these people can be difficult due to the social and cultural tendency to hide such conditions and the fact that some disabilities cannot be easily seen from the outside. With this situation in mind, Dentsu Advertising launched the “Think Universal” project, which uses visual stimuli to depict the existence of these disabilities and draw public attention. The tool "Think Box" enables people to experience various illnesses and physical impairments in order to deepen their understanding of them. To attract attention and arouse curiosity, the project's exterior is colored in bright red or light pink and the interior is filled with small colored squares.

55

Animal Cards

Studio: Coton Design
Designer: Hiroko Sakai

C:0 M:43 Y:35 K:0
R:244 G:170 B:150

C:0 M:85 Y:99 K:0
R:233 G:71 B:12

C:46 M:15 Y:56 K:11
R:142 G:172 B:122

C:57 M:2 Y:79 K:0
R:119 G:189 B:91

C:91 M:20 Y:3 K:0
R:0 G:145 B:212

C:7 M:23 Y:85 K:0
R:240 G:200 B:48

Idea: Mix and match colors for adding interest

The Animal Cards project was originally started by Studio Couche, a children's photography studio. The designers set out to create a toy that both parents and children could enjoy. It is a combination of cut-out animal-shaped envelopes and animal character cards. The designer chose 4 animals (cow, zebra, tiger and leopard) and 6 colorful envelopes. When the envelopes and cards are correctly matched, the corresponding animals are revealed. Even the wrong combination can produce interesting effects.

56

Posters for the 2013 World Table Tennis Championships

Studio: Dentsu
Designer: Yuri Uenish

Idea: Fluorescent lines for a stronger visual effect

In 2013, designer Yuri Uenish collaborated with "The Ping Pong Club", a famous table tennis manga in Japan, to create these posters. The designer used 2 fluorescent lines to express gradient graphics. The strong contrast between the colors and lines, along with the fame of the manga characters, makes the posters memorable.

C:65 M:12 Y:4 K:0
R:74 G:176 B:223

C:11 M:81 Y:0 K:0
R:216 G:77 B:150

C:57 M:73 Y:0 K:0
R:130 G:85 B:160

57

C:30 M:85 Y:87 K:0
R:194 G:72 B:49

C:76 M:13 Y:90 K:0
R:37 G:166 B:76

C:4 M:46 Y:91 K:0
R:247 G:162 B:17

C:0 M:52 Y:15 K:0
R:255 G:158 B:178

C:52 M:0 Y:33 K:0
R:132 G:210 B:194

C:38 M:73 Y:65 K:0
R:178 G:96 B:84

C:90 M:93 Y:13 K:0
R:61 G:48 B:138

2019 Calendar

Studio: Kata Kata

Idea: A colorful nature scene

This is an A2-sized calendar designed by Kata Kata. The animals of the Chinese zodiac are the focus of the poster. As 2019 was the Year of the Pig, Kata Kata depicted a family of wild boars running around a farm as well as the beauty of nature, conveying the desire for everyone's life to be as colorful as the picture.

58

Made in Hokkaido

Studio: Dentsu
Designers: Aya Yagi, Kayoko Shimoyama, Kumiku Shiraki
Art Director: Aya Yagi
Creative Director: Nobuaki Hattori

こんなものがあるんだ。
って、言わせたい。

北海道には、ゆたかな自然がある。
北海道には、おいしいものがたくさんある。
それは、日本人なら、もうだれもが知っていること。
でも、それだけで良いのでしょうか。
この土地には、まだまだ、たくさんの魅力が眠っています。
ここで暮らしてはじめてわかる、北海道。
知れば知るほど、想像以上に広くて深い、北海道。
地元で愛されている商品こそ、本当に伝えたい、
この土地の魅力があるのではないでしょうか。
生産者の想いや商品を発掘し、東京の皆さまに伝える
「北海道ブランド発信プロジェクト」。
これからも、わたしたちは、ひとつひとつ丁寧に、
北海道のあたらしい魅力を育てていきます。

made in
北海道

北海道ブランド発信PROJECT

Idea: Match colors with local features

Hokkaido is the largest and northernmost administrative region in Japan and has many attractions, but it is not particularly popular. Therefore, the Hokkaido Brand Information Project was established to introduce its charms throughout Japan. As part of the project, an event called "Made in Hokkaido" was held in Tokyo to sell items from Hokkaido. The logo for the event consists of patterns of Hokkaido's natural scenery. To reflect the natural features of Hokkaido with its mountains and ocean, the colors of the poster are mostly a vivid dark blue and emerald green.

59

Arashiyama Chirin

Studio: SQUEEZE Inc.
Designer: Miki Terada
Photographer: Tomoko Kawai

C:50 M:4 Y:3 K:0
R:128 G:201 B:236

Idea: Consistency in colors for a whole set

Arashiyama Chirin is a dried fish shop specializing in dried whitebait and is located in Arashiyama, Kyoto. In the past, the majority of its customers were of an older generation. In order to break through its sales bottleneck, the shop decided to create a new brand image with the aim of attracting younger customers. The shop invited SQUEEZE Inc. to create a new packaging design for its products. Based on the new brand vision, Arashiyama Chirin developed new flavors of dried whitebait. For the 16 new flavors, SQUEEZE Inc. designed 16 small packages in different colors and patterns, each one showcasing the corresponding flavor — Japanese pepper, curry, rice cake, black pepper, etc. For the outer packaging, the lovely and fresh colors of blue and white were chosen.

Koeido Takeda Wagashi

Studio: CIFAKA, Inc.
Designers: Daisuke Sakumoto, Sachiyo Sunada
Illustrator: Noritake
Art Director: Daisuke Sakumoto
Photographer: Shinichiro Uchida

Idea: Use illustrations and color matching to create an overall lovely tone

Koeido has a time-honored history of producing wagashi, an iconic souvenir from Okayama, Japan. The studio wanted to design impressive and high-quality packaging to highlight the identity of the creator. Therefore, the studio entrusted Noritake, with his simple but expressive style, to draw the illustrations.

Wagashi is a Japanese dessert that finds its origin in the Japanese folk tale *Momotaro Densetsu*. The studio commissioned Noritake to draw a harmonious scene where Momotaro, his friends and his enemies all come together. In order to keep the overall tone balanced, the studio chose light pink and yellow to match the cute illustrations.

C:10 M:31 Y:53 K:0
R:231 G:187 B:127

C:10 M:30 Y0 K:0
R:229 G:194 B:219

C:10 M:13 Y:22 K:0
R:234 G:223 B:202

61

Clip Family

Studio: Sugai World Inc.
Designer: Yu Sugai

C:76 M:43 Y:11 K:0
R:61 G:126 B:180

C:6 M:85 Y:31 K:0
R:223 G:68 B:114

C:7 M:55 Y:61 K:0
R:230 G:140 B:95

Idea: Combining monochromes to create a sense of playfulness

This set of handy clips can be used both as regular clips or as bookmarks. They can be bent and placed in water for up to 5 minutes. The clips can be used to hold book pages as well as be used as a hook when placed on a pen. The clips are made from environmentally friendly materials, 95% of which are natural fibers.

The wrapping paper of each clip uses a different color according to the image of the clip: Blue is used for the image of a boy, pink for the image of a girl and orange for the image of a cat. The various colors make the white clips livelier and playful.

Hello! We are
Clip family!

Mew !

Mew !

I can Fly!

Hoho !

Nice !
columbia rd

僕ら、コーディネイトの天才なのさ。
みためも、うまうま。
しろくまのお米
www.niigata-shirokuma.jp
しろくまのお米
検索

C:15 M:30 Y:45 K:0
R:221 G:186 B:143

C:11 M:41 Y:88 K:0
R:227 G:165 B:42

C:9 M:18 Y:88 K:0
R:238 G:207 B:36

C:9 M:87 Y:93 K:0
R:220 G:66 B:31

C:84 M:61 Y:55 K:15
R:48 G:87 B:97

62

Shirokuma No Okome

Studio: Frame Inc.
Designer: Ryuta Ishikawa

Idea: Creating warmth from colors

This Japanese rice brand design adopts the figure of a polar bear as its trademark, with rice as the bear's nose. The brownish-yellow background conveys a feeling of warmth and softness, while the white polar bear and the delicate shapes of rice show the purity and cleanliness of the rice.

PANTASTIC!! 2018 SPRING

おいしいパンとパンにまつわる生活の提案
パンタスティック!!
2018 AUTUMN at PARCO
パパパパン!
11.2(fri) → 11.12(mon)
会場：広島PARCO 本館6F・パルコファクトリー
[入場無料]
お問合せ先
広島PARCO 082-542-2111(代表)
詳しい情報はこちらをチェック!
facebookページ[パンタスティック!!]
instagram[@pantastic_papapapan]

PANTASTIC!! 2018 AUTUMN

Shimokitazawa Film

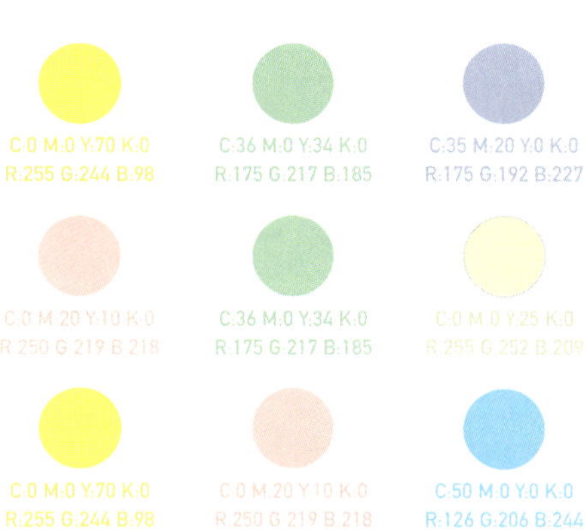

63

Takahashi Yuki Series

Illustrator: Takahashi Yuki

Idea: Cute pink hue

Takahashi Yuki is an illustrator and active member of Conico. In 2016, her book *Coffee & Bread* was published by the Korean bookstore Your Mind. In 2017, Japanese bookstore and gallery On Reading published a collection of her work called *New Teleportation* under their label ELVIS PRESS. Today she is active in various media industries such as books, magazines, advertisements and CD jackets. Takahashi Yuki's works have a feminine style that is rich in color. The pink hue reflects the girly and cute side of the illustrator.

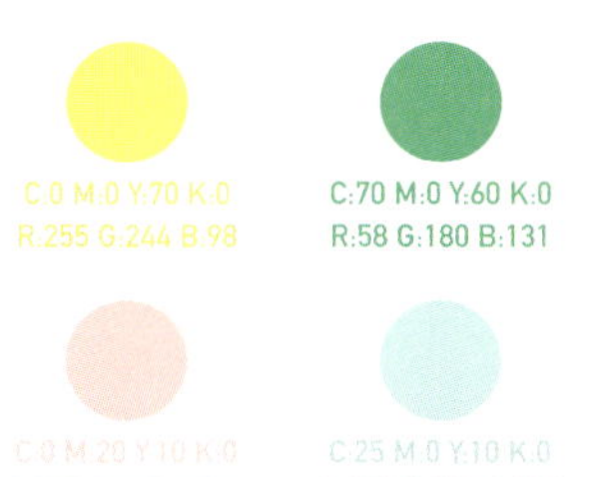

C:0 M:0 Y:70 K:0
R:255 G:244 B:98

C:70 M:0 Y:60 K:0
R:58 G:180 B:131

C:35 M:20 Y:0 K:0
R:175 G:192 B:227

C:0 M:20 Y:10 K:0
R:250 G:219 B:218

C:25 M:0 Y:10 K:0
R:200 G:231 B:233

C:35 M:20 Y:0 K:0
R:175 G:192 B:227

Life is Beautiful

Gift tora no maki

64

Sanuki Mulberry Tea

Studio: Studio Bus Stop
Art Director: Shinichi Kuroda
Creative Director: Takeshi Nishimori
Photographer: Ken Yamauchi

C:24 M:15 Y:85 K:0
R:207 G:200 B:59

C:7 M:49 Y:54 K:0
R:231 G:153 B:112

C:43 M:6 Y:19 K:0
R:155 G:204 B:208

C:79 M:27 Y:100 K:0
R:46 G:141 B:58

Idea: A simple background color embellished with bright colors

Mulberry leaves are produced in Kagawa Prefecture, Japan, which is where the name "Sanuki Mulberry Tea" comes from. The image on the package is that of the local producer, Obachan (the Japanese pronunciation for "aunt"). The different packaging represents the different product usage. The packaging has a white or wood-colored background, which allows the cute image of "Obachan" to be brought out in the green tea leaves and pink, orange, yellow and blue apron.

Behavior Norms Posters

Studios: Asatsu-DK Inc., NesT.O. Inc.
Designers: Ryu Yokoyama, Yasuko Matsuo, Yu Nagaba
Illustrator: Yu Nagaba
Art Directors: Fusanari Masuda, Naoko Fujihira
Creative Director: Mari Hosokawa

メトロ文化財団

あなたのマナー、
いいカンジ!?
Are your manners in good shape?

声

【こえ voice】
車内での会話は、
声の大きさにご注意ください。
Please be considerate of others when talking on the subway.

メトロ文化財団
あなたのマナー、
いいカンジ!?
Are your manners in good shape?
列
【れつ line】
ご乗車の際は、
列に並んで順序よく。
Please wait in line and board the train
in an orderly manner.

あなたのマナー、
いいカンジ!?
Are your manners in good shape?
メトロ文化財団
優
【ゆう kindness】
優先席では、必要としている方へ
席をお譲りください。
Please offer priority seats to passengers who may need them.

メトロ文化財団
あなたのマナー、
いいカンジ!?
Are your manners in good shape?
走
【はしる run】
ストップかけこみ乗車！危険な
だけでなく、電車の遅れの原因に。
Don't run onto the train!
Not only is it dangerous to yourself and others, it leads to delays.

メトロ文化財団
あなたのマナー、
いいカンジ!?
Are your manners in good shape?
滴
【しずく drop】
雨の日は、濡れた傘の
取り扱いにご配慮を。
bothersome to others.

メトロ文化財団

あなたのマナー、
いいカンジ!?

Are your manners in good shape?

【すわる sit】
座席の幅とりは、まわりの方
の迷惑に。ご配慮ください。

Please make room for as many passengers to sit as possible.

Idea: Use light tones to reduce the sense of seriousness

The phrase “behavior norms” usually reminds people of seriousness and responsibility. However, the design of this behavior norms poster tries to avoid these concepts and instead conjures feelings of humor and affability through illustrations and the adoption of gentle and fresh pink tones.

C:36 M:0 Y:11 K:0
R:166 G:241 B:247

C:9 M:58 Y:51 K:0
R:234 G:138 B:113

C:58 M:0 Y:38 K:0
R:81 G:231 B:196

C:10 M:0 Y:84 K:0
R:249 G:242 B:30

C:35 M:43 Y:51 K:0
R:182 G:151 B:123

C:44 M:50 Y:0 K:0
R:164 G:136 B:211

Furoshiki with Animals

Studio: Cochae

Creative Directors: Toshiko Ohashi, Kensuke Kawamura

Idea: Gentle color combinations with cartoon animals

The design concept of this furoshiki series is "tie fun, spread fun and wrap fun". The furoshiki has patterns of 4 cats or dogs. Different animal images will appear depending on the way the furoshiki is folded. The corners of the furoshiki can be knotted to create the ears or tails of cats and dogs. Soft and sweet tones complement the cute animal patterns, making this furoshiki particularly attractive to women and children. Use it to wrap gifts or lunch boxes and take your "cat" or "dog" with you!

小袖ようかん
くり
小袖ようかん
本ねり
小袖ようかん
抹茶
小袖ようかん
おぐら
小袖ようかん
黒ごま

おわせ最中
くり
おわせ最中
おぐら

67

Red-bean Yokan

Designer: Masaki Fukumori

Idea: Match colors and flavors

Yokan is a Japanese dessert made of sweetened red bean paste. This series uses traditional Japanese patterns and colors on the packaging to match the different flavors: brown for chestnut, purple for original, green for matcha, pink for red bean and blue for black sesame.

C:14 M:29 Y:83 K:0
R:233 G:191 B:53

C:42 M:44 Y:0 K:0
R:170 G:149 B:224

C:44 M:27 Y:82 K:0
R:164 G:172 B:73

C:17 M:64 Y:29 K:0
R:220 G:123 B:143

C:60 M:36 Y:28 K:0
R:118 G:149 B:170

Kata Kata × Musubi Furoshiki Cooperative Project

Studio: Kata Kata

Idea: Colors that represent natural delight

Kata Kata uses traditional Japanese dyeing and selected printing techniques to create original fabric products. They draw inspiration from things in daily life, such as animals, insects, plants and scenery. As a result, they tend to choose natural colors like grass green and water blue. Kata Kata integrates their own stories into the designs of the products and hopes people will feel a sense of warmth and delight and use their imagination when enjoying the products. This furoshiki is manufactured by Musubi, a renowned traditional dye manufacturer in Kyoto.

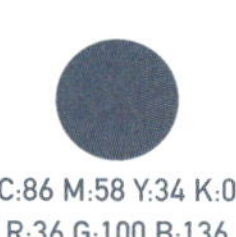

C:86 M:58 Y:34 K:0
R:36 G:100 B:136

C:93 M:85 Y:58 K:34
R:27 G:45 B:69

C:27 M:24 Y:17 K:0
R:196 G:191 B:198

C:73 M:52 Y:100 K:15
R:81 G:102 B:46

C:10 M:20 Y:18 K:0
R:232 G:211 B:202

C:59 M:65 Y:75 K:16
R:115 G:89 B:68

C:50 M:43 Y:40 K:0
R:145 G:141 B:141

C:19 M:33 Y:78 K:0
R:214 G:175 B:73

C:73 M:48 Y:99 K:9
R:84 G:111 B:50

C:27 M:100 Y:99 K:0
R:189 G:26 B:34

C:60 M:48 Y:100 K:5
R:121 G:121 B:45

C:56 M:11 Y:27 K:0
R:117 G:184 B:188

C:16 M:70 Y:84 K:0
R:212 G:105 B:50

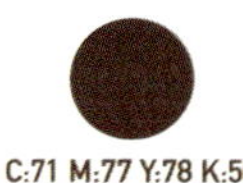

C:71 M:77 Y:78 K:50
R:62 G:44 B:39

69

Sumo Animals Packaging

Studio: Ono and Associates Inc.
Designer: Ayako Ono

Idea: A non-conventional choice of colors

This gift box is used to pack rice crackers. Paper figures of sumo animals are included in the box, so customers can enjoy the fun of the product even after the rice crackers have been eaten. Small items that would have been discarded are given a second life. The animals do not necessarily have their own natural colors, as the designer has chosen a variety of colors for their skins and clothing to give them a more amusing appearance.

C:74 M:76 Y:17 K:0
R:92 G:77 B:140

C:24 M:3 Y:75 K:0
R:208 G:219 B:89

70

Nagasaki-no Neco

Designer: Nobuyuki Matsumoto

C:90 M:80 Y:20 K:0
R:45 G:68 B:134

C:14 M:17 Y:70 K:0
R:227 G:206 B:96

C:54 M:94 Y:75 K:25
R:117 G:38 B:52

C:85 M:54 Y:82 K:21
R:38 G:90 B:65

Idea: Express emotions through colors

Established in 2016, Nagasaki-no Neco is a souvenir shop selling cat-themed products in the heart of Nagasaki Prefecture. There are many cats in Nagasaki Prefecture. The majority of these cats have a kink in their tails, so they are known as "bent-tailed cats". The owner and designer of the shop, Nobuyuki Matsumoto, has created a variety of products and shop logos based on the characteristics of these cats. Each product uses only 1 or 2 colors, such as white, black, orange, green and yellow. These bright and vibrant colors are combined with the image of cats to give a direct visual impression of the cats' characteristics, such as lively, funny, relaxed and easy-going. The designer also hopes to express his passion for changing the living conditions of stray cats through these vibrant colors.

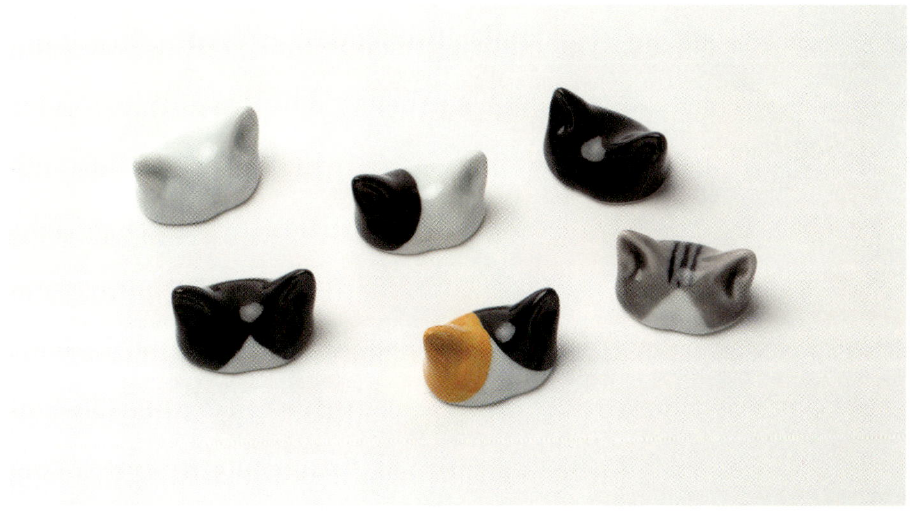

71

Fun Origami

Studio: Cochae
Designers: Yosuke Jikuhara, Miki Takeda

Idea: Colors create endless possibilities

Miki Takeda and Yosuke Jikuhara have worked together to set up the Cochae Design Studio. They draw inspiration from traditional Japanese toys and cartoon characters to design origami in a novel way. Cochae, the name of the studio, comes from a folk song in Miki and Yosuke's hometown of Okayama. It means "welcome first-time visitors". Cochae's interesting interpretation of origami keeps this traditional art form alive in a unique way.

Cochae uses the design concept of "new shoots from old trees" to integrate origami with traditional Japanese folk toys such as puppet dolls and Daruma dolls and traditional Kyoto characters. By infusing the elements of traditional characters into origami, people can both enjoy the fun of origami as well as appreciate the traditional culture of this art form. The rich variety and unique patterns of Cochae's origami are so different from traditional origami that you will never feel bored. The designs of Cochae's origami showcase endless possibilities. You can fold a piece of paper printed with patterns into a variety of shapes by following simple steps.

THE ORIGINAL OF THE GRAPHIC ORIGAMI
古典おりがみ
元祖絵付折紙シリーズ第３弾!
1921年発行の『チエノ折紙』を大胆にアレンジしたコチャエの定番!
2004年の発行から愛されてきた古典シリーズが堂々リニューアル!
伝承折紙をベースにしているので楽しみながら日本文化を知ることができます!
鶴 Crane
亀 Turtle
兜 Helmet
蛙 Frog
蝉 Cicada
6 種類 (135mm × 135mm) 各 3 枚／全 18 枚 + 折図付
6 types (135mm × 135mm) each 3 / all 18 + diagram
MADE IN JAPAN
design by COCHAE
4 573231 340024
COCHAE
戦前折紙 古典おりがみ

72

Koten

Studio: Cochae
Photographer: Harumi Obama

Idea: Contrasting gold with bright colors

Chieno origami first appeared in the 1920s and 1930s and mainly bases its themes on traditional Japanese symbols, including cranes, turtles, frogs and omamori (blessing amulets). In addition to these elements, this origami set also incorporates new Cochae designs: helmets and cicadas. The folded origami can be placed in the packaging box. The whole box is gold, which creates a sharp contrast with the brightly colored origami in the box.

C:20 M:27 Y:93 K:0
R:214 G:183 B:27

C:0 M:82 Y:78 K:0
R:234 G:80 B:52

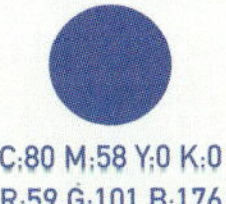

C:80 M:58 Y:0 K:0
R:59 G:101 B:176

C:66 M:0 Y:85 K:0
R:86 G:181 B:82

C:7 M:9 Y:86 K:0
R:244 G:223 B:42

73

Tree Rain Wear

Studio: E. Co., Ltd.
Designer: Yoshihiko Masuyama
Art Director: Kenichi Matsumot

Idea: Strong color palettes create a positive atmosphere

This raincoat can be folded up into a leaf-like package. With a design concept of "humans are part of nature", the raincoat was designed to transform the melancholy image of rain into something positive. The use of colors such as bright yellow, red and dark green also helps to emphasize a positive and interesting atmosphere.

C:78 M:21 Y:60 K:0
R:29 G:150 B:122

C:0 M:20 Y:70 K:0
R:253 G:211 B:92

C:0 M:83 Y:73 K:0
R:233 G:77 B:59

Tree Rain Wear
Tree Rain Wear
Tree Rain Wear

アバンギャルド

Avant-garde

Chapter

4

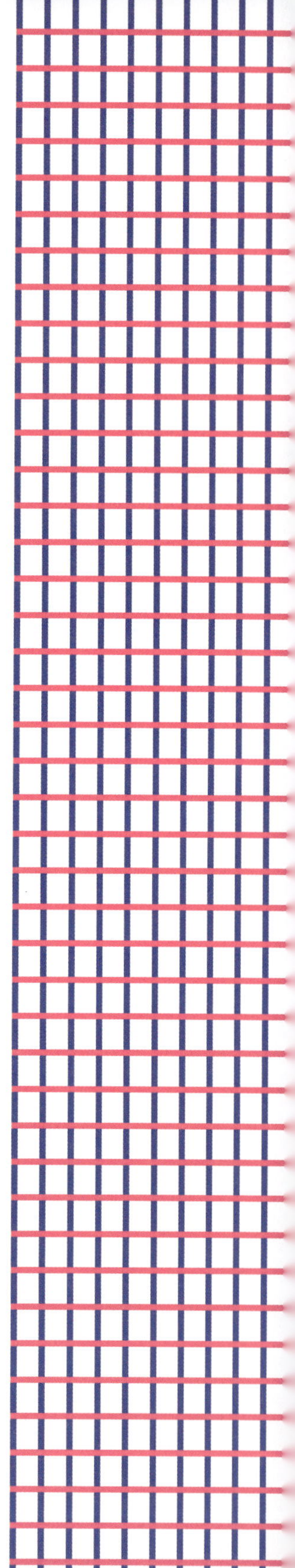

○ Multiple bright colors in one picture/ ○ Extremely gaudy colors/ ○ Colors and lines interact to create strong visual effects/ ○ Light tones reduce the heaviness of themes/ ○ A bright Kawaii color scheme creates a vivid, childish style/ ○ Weird shapes and colors/ ○ Lively scheme with bright colors creates a sense of fashion/ ○ Use a bright color scheme to attract attention/ ○ A bright and vivid color scheme/ ○ Bold color blocking/ ○ Creating psychological suggestions through colors/ ○ Large background with bright colors/ ○ Collision of muted colors/ ○ Color blocks collide to strengthen visual effect/ ○ Eye-catching fluorescent colors/ ○ Rotating colorful patterns/ ○ Using plain background colors to emphasize the subject/ ○ Placid colors accentuate fluorescent blue/ ○ Unusual choice in background colors/ ○ Messy but beautiful colors

74

Waka Graphics

Studio: AYOND
Designer: Shun Sasaki

三輪の山　かに待ち見む
年経とも　たづぬる人も　あらじと思へば

伊勢

訳　最果タヒ

待っていると言えるのは、あなたがわたしを好きな場合で、待っていると言えるのは、あなたの恋が変わらぬ場合で、何年経とうと来ることはない、そうわかっていながら「待つ」と、待つとわたしが言うそのとき、それを聞くのはわたし一人だ、わたしはわたしに待つと、待てばと、待ちますと、くりかえして突き刺すのです。
三輪山。まだわたしを愛しているなら待っていますからと、誰かが誰かへ歌った場所で、呻いています。わたしは、あなたを待ってしまいます。

C:0 M:0 Y:0 K:70
R:114 G:113 B:113

C:85 M:53 Y:0 K:0
R:20 G:106 B:181

C:0 M:91 Y:16 K:0
R:230 G:45 B:123

C:0 M:0 Y:0 K:20
R:220 G:221 B:221

C:24 M:0 Y:91 K:0
R:209 G:221 B:33

C:73 M:0 Y:83 K:0
R:47 G:175 B:88

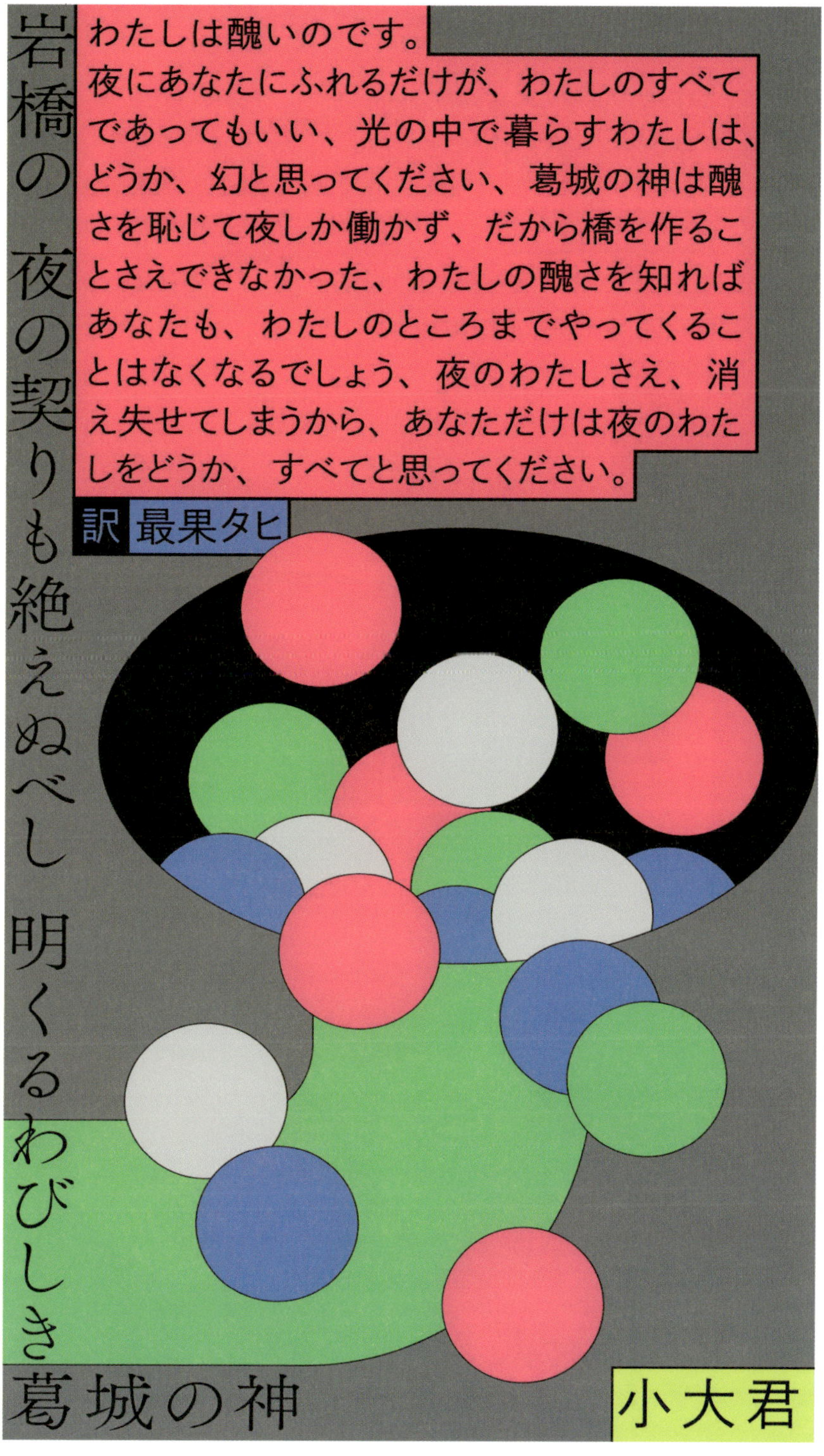

岩橋の 夜の契りも絶えぬべし 明くるわびしき 葛城の神

わたしは醜いのです。
夜にあなたにふれるだけが、わたしのすべてであってもいい、光の中で暮らすわたしは、どうか、幻と思ってください、葛城の神は醜さを恥じて夜しか働かず、だから橋を作ることさえできなかった、わたしの醜さを知ればあなたも、わたしのところまでやってくることはなくなるでしょう、夜のわたしさえ、消え失せてしまうから、あなただけは夜のわたしをどうか、すべてと思ってください。

訳 最果タヒ

小大君

訳 最果タヒ
いつのまにか、
琴の音色に松の葉のこすれる音が重なって、
いつからだろう、どの音だろう、
松の風が張られた琴は、どの弦から鳴り響いたのだろう、
未来へとばかり流れる音楽に、身を、ゆだねながら遡る。
斎宮女御
琴の音に
峯の松風かよふらし
いづれの緒より
しらべそめけむ

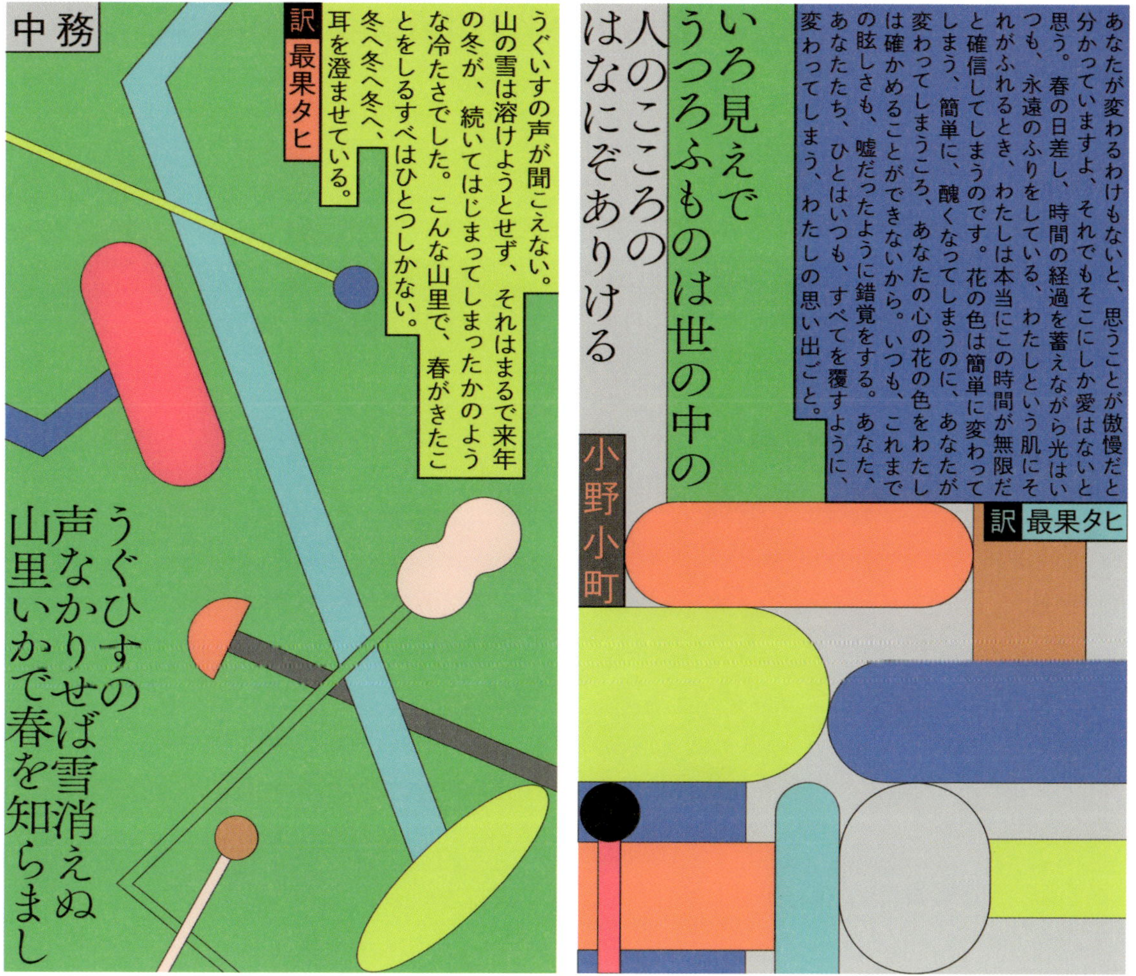

Idea: Multiple bright colors in one picture

The designer has transformed the poetry of Tahi Saihate into dynamic posters overflowing with modernism to interpret the works from a modern perspective.

75

Art Works by Tadanori Yokoo

Artist: Tadanori Yokoo

A LA MAISON DE M. CIVEÇAWA
1965
US Garumera Chamber of Commerce in Ankuku Butoh school
1030mm × 728mm
MoMA

C:3 M:40 Y:91 K:0
R:242 G:171 B:22

C:0 M:100 Y:100 K:0
R:230 G:0 B:18

C:71 M:14 Y:50 K:0
R:64 G:165 B:143

C:94 M:43 Y:5 K:0
R:0 G:116 B:186

Moat
1966
455mm × 530mm
Tokushima Modern Art Museum

Idea: Extremely gaudy colors

C:3 M:78 Y:19 K:0
R:229 G:88 B:134

C:87 M:54 Y:7 K:0
R:0 G:104 B:172

Tadanori Yokoo, a famous Japanese artist whose works are hung and collected in numerous art museums all over the world, was born in Hyogo Prefecture in 1936. In 1972, he held a solo exhibition at the Museum of Modern Art in New York. After this, he was invited to attend biennials in Paris, Venice, Sao Paulo and other places, winning high commendation internationally. He established the Tadanori Yokoo Museum of Contemporary Art in Kobe in 2012 and the Teshima Yokoo House in Kagawa in 2013. Tadanori Yokoo has won numerous awards including the Mainichi Design Award, 1995; the Medal with Purple Ribbon, 2001; the Order of the Rising Sun, Gold Rays with Rosette and the Asahi Prize, 2011; and the 27th Praemium Imperiale, 2015.

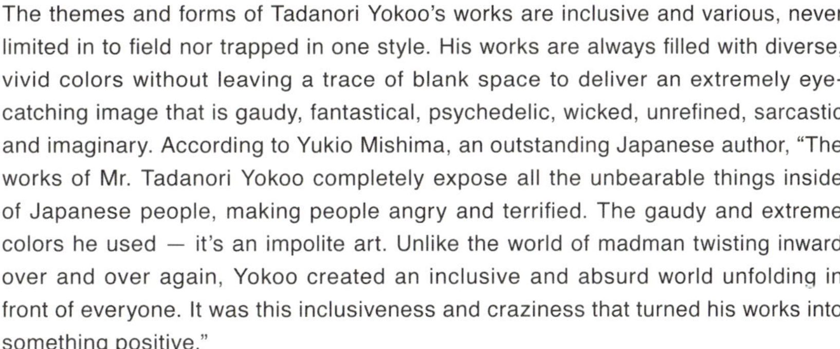

The themes and forms of Tadanori Yokoo's works are inclusive and various, never limited in to field nor trapped in one style. His works are always filled with diverse, vivid colors without leaving a trace of blank space to deliver an extremely eye-catching image that is gaudy, fantastical, psychedelic, wicked, unrefined, sarcastic and imaginary. According to Yukio Mishima, an outstanding Japanese author, "The works of Mr. Tadanori Yokoo completely expose all the unbearable things inside of Japanese people, making people angry and terrified. The gaudy and extreme colors he used — it's an impolite art. Unlike the world of madman twisting inward over and over again, Yokoo created an inclusive and absurd world unfolding in front of everyone. It was this inclusiveness and craziness that turned his works into something positive."

Koshimaki-osen
1966
Condition Troupe
1030 mm × 728 mm
MoMA

C:0 M:74 Y:3 K:0
R:234 G:99 B:157

C:94 M:33 Y:8 K:0
R:0 G:128 B:192

C:0 M:46 Y:98 K:0
R:244 G:160 B:0

C:0 M:99 Y:88 K:0
R:230 G:8 B:35

C:79 M:38 Y:82 K:8
R:53 G:122 B:77

TADANORI YOKOO
The poster that Tadanori Yokoo designed for himself

C:69 M:6 Y:5 K:0
R:37 G:179 B:226

C:0 M:99 Y:98 K:0
R:230 G:8 B:20

C:0 M:58 Y:4 K:0
R:239 G:139 B:178

C:0 M:38 Y:92 K:0
R:247 G:176 B:9

C:81 M:30 Y:74 K:0
R:28 G:137 B:96

76

Graphic Trial

Designer: Kazunari Hattori

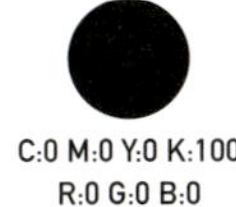

C:0 M:0 Y:0 K:100
R:0 G:0 B:0

C:0 M:0 Y:100 K:0
R:255 G:241 B:0

C:100 M:0 Y:0 K:0
R:0 G:160 B:233

C:0 M:100 Y:0 K:0
R:228 G:0 B:127

graphic trial vol.2 designed by kazunari hattori printed by graphic arts center, toppan, 2007

Idea: Colors and lines interact to create strong visual effects

This series of posters was created by Japanese graphic designer Kazunari Hattori during a graphic experiment focused on printing. Printing is usually adopted to represent graphic art, but Hattori wanted to go a different direction by making printing itself the focus. Hattori was familiar with how CMYK color points present in printing and wanted to make an unconventional attempt during his experiment. He decided to replace dots with lines to present the color and gradation of the print. After he hand-painted the lines and printed them in CMYK colors, a series of textured color charts was created. These clearly showed the gradient of different colors. Enjoying his project, Hattori began to conceive of using flags as patterns to present lines. He said: "Generally speaking, graphic works are the main character, and printed CMYK dots exist only to present those works. But in this experiment, the CMYK lines are the protagonist, and the flag was created to present this theme." Variations in line thickness and spacing were also included as part of the experiment and demonstrated a change in the tone.

77

Boundary

Designer: Taro Uryu

C:85 M:50 Y:0 K:0
R:3 G:110 B:184

C:0 M:12 Y:3 K:0
R:252 G:235 B:239

Idea: Light tones reduce the heaviness of themes

This advertisement was designed by Taro Uryu for a performance at a small theater, Yarinage. In order to show the ambiguous boundaries of biology (including that of human beings), a pen was given to a small African ape resembling a chimpanzee as the sign of communication. This reinforces the ambiguities differentiating apes and human beings. In addition, the designer added the Chinese characters " 境界 " to the poster. The circular frame and inclining stroke of " 曰 " in " 境 " implies that "there is no entrance", and the " 田 " in " 界 " was designed in a cross formation meaning "forbidden". All of the strokes in these 2 characters were presented with dotted lines, further emphasizing the sense of ambiguity. Despite the heavy topic of the performance, the designer hoped that the audience could watch it with interest as a form of entertainment. To create this feeling, the designer used simple lines and soft, light tones to reduce the heaviness of the theme.

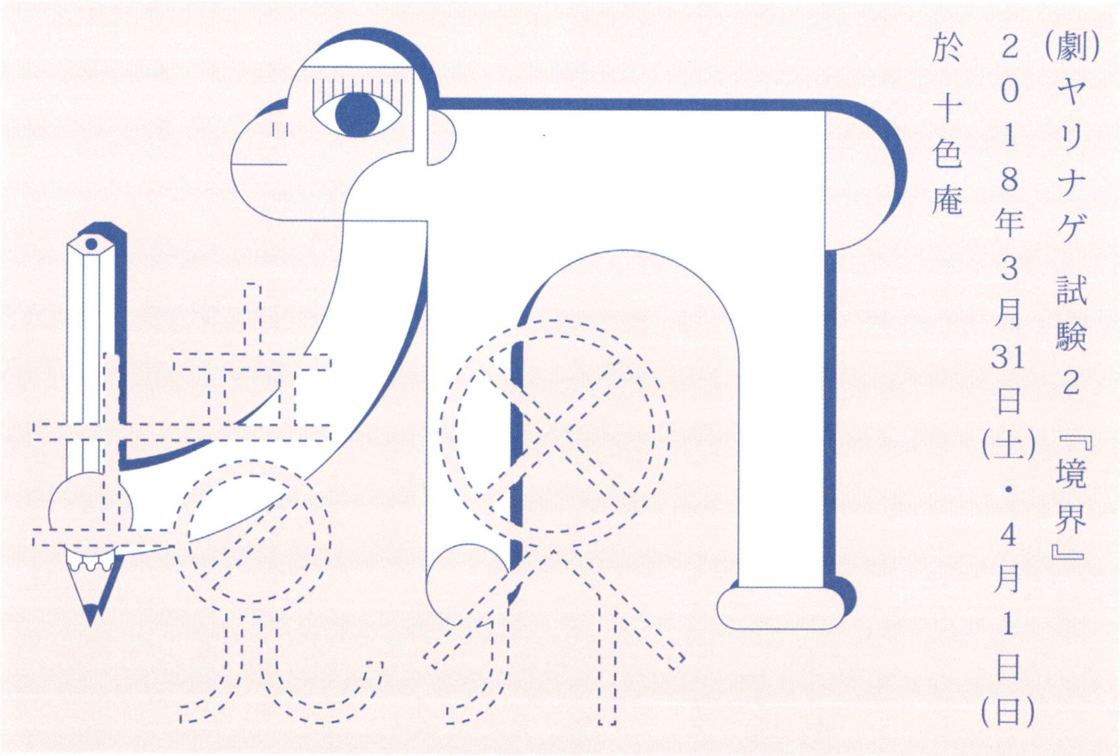

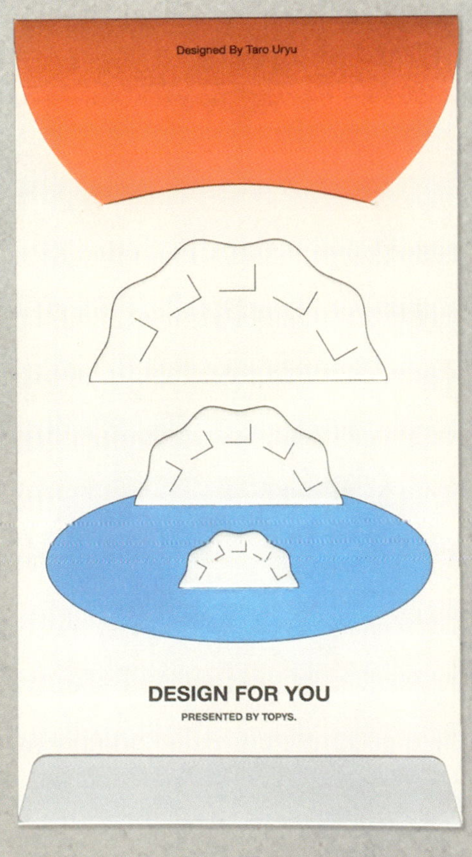

78

C:71 M:14 Y:0 K:0
R:34 G:168 B:225

C:0 M:78 Y:67 K:0
R:234 G:90 B:70

C:25 M:19 Y:14 K:0
R:200 G:201 B:208

C:7 M:7 Y:7 K:0
R:240 G:237 B:236

Red Packet Project

Designer: Taro Uryu

Idea: A bright Kawaii color scheme creates a vivid, childish style

The designer created a red envelope design for the "Celebrate the New Year" project conducted by the Chinese creative website TOPYS. The dumpling-shaped skirt was printed using embossing technology. Since the envelope is meant to be given to young people during the celebration, designers tried to use bright Kawaii colors and geometric figures to create a cool and amusing style.

79

HELLO TAIPEI

Designer: Taro Uryu

Idea: Weird shapes and colors

This is the Taipei version of a postcard presented by the designer while selling magazines at a book exhibition held at pon ding (朋丁), a collaborative space for events, in Taipei, China. On the postcard is a woman with an orange "missile"-shaped hairstyle wearing a "Xiaolongbao (small steamed bun) dress" standing on gradient blue shadows, with a scarlet sans serif font placed on the top of the images. The whole image conveys the designer's idea of a unique, elegant and quirky fashion sense.

80

What Shall We Eat Today?

Designer: Taro Uryu

Idea: Lively scheme with bright colors creates a sense of fashion

This work is entitled "Burger Day" and was part of the illustration project "What shall we eat today?" displayed in the Japanese electronic *GAP 1969* magazine. Respecting the overall type and style of this brand, the designer gave this illustration a sense of fashion and understandability without making it excessively abstract. The designer chose lively, bright colors to express the style and characteristics of the brand.

C:5 M:30 Y:45 K:0
R:240 G:193 B:143

C:0 M:21 Y:19 K:0
R:250 G:216 B:201

C:0 M:100 Y:100 K:0
R:230 G:0 B:18

C:100 M:0 Y:0 K:0
R:0 G:160 B:233

C:50 M:0 Y:100 K:0
R:143 G:195 B:31

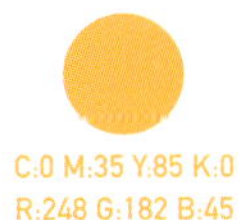

C:0 M:35 Y:85 K:0
R:248 G:182 B:45

81

2018 NU Chayamachi Summer Sale

Designer: Makoto Yamaguchi
Art Director: Koji Sasaki
Creative Director: Censure Urushizaki
Illustrator: Nimura Daisuke

Idea: Use a bright color scheme to attract attention

As the seasons change, NU Chayamachi enters its third year of displaying illustrated sale advertisements. The third edition of the ad differs from typical printed advertisements as it is spread through the Internet and digital cinema. In order to meet the demands for animated effects, the illustrator designed a girl dancing freely and duplicated this image as the visual subject in the ad. A large area of bright yellow was used as the background to attract attention. The girl's clothing is also done in bright hues of blue and rose red to match the bright background.

C:0 M:0 Y:100 K:0
R:255 G:241 B:0

C:0 M:90 Y:0 K:0
R:230 G:46 B:139

C:100 M:0 Y:0 K:0
R:0 G:160 B:233

82

A Mysterious and Little Bit Boring Daily Life

Designer: Tomomi Mizukoshi

Idea: A bright and vivid color scheme

The designer is inspired by her everyday life, from the plants along the street to stray cats in the parking lot of a construction site, so she often looks unconsciously for interesting things to paint while she walks. The themes of her works come from her usual sketches and photos. She will also work with illustrators to create an image. Image creation is the most interesting part of the painting process. These simple but vivid images almost always lead her to a deeper world. She believes that the combination of colors, images and themes plays a key role in concept creation. The cats and dogs shown in the pictures, with their bright, vivid colors, can bring people joy and temporarily liberate them from a boring and exhausting life.

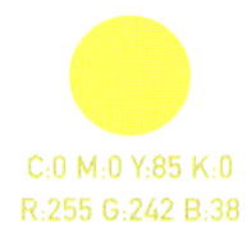
C:0 M:0 Y:85 K:0
R:255 G:242 B:38

C:57 M:0 Y:0 K:0
R:98 G:198 B:242

C:0 M:18 Y:0 K:0
R:251 G:224 B:236

C:0 M:53 Y:100 K:0
R:242 G:145 B:0

C:0 M:100 Y:51 K:0
R:229 G:0 B:78

C:68 M:32 Y:0 K:0
R:81 G:146 B:207

C:0 M:20 Y:0 K:0
R:250 G:220 B:233

C:29 M:0 Y:0 K:0
R:189 G:228 B:249

C:9 M:47 Y:100 K:0
R:230 G:153 B:0

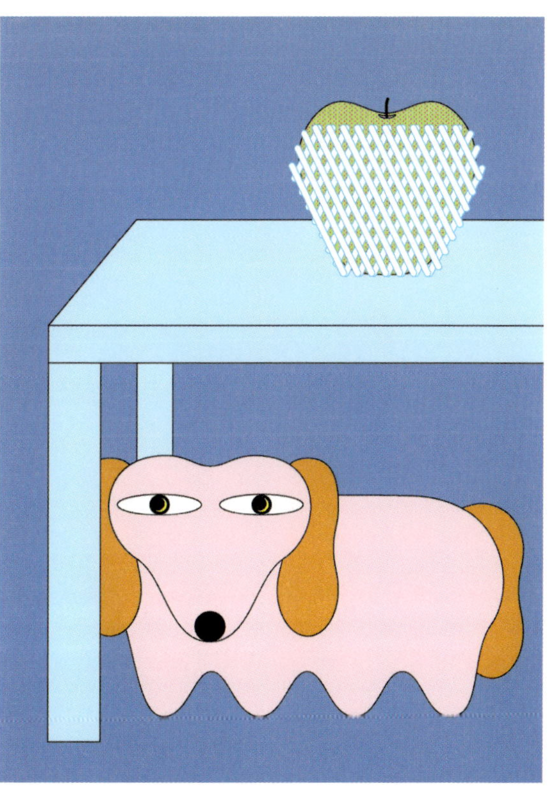

C:38 M:0 Y:11 K:0
R:167 G:218 B:229

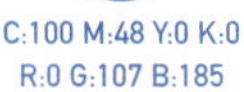

C:100 M:48 Y:0 K:0
R:0 G:107 B:185

C:0 M:95 Y:100 K:0
R:231 G:36 B:16

C:100 M:59 Y:0 K:0
R:0 G:93 B:173

C:0 M:71 Y:100 K:0
R:237 G:106 B:0

C:39 M:0 Y:100 K:0
R:173 G:206 B:0

C:95 M:0 Y:100 K:0
R:0 G:156 B:66

C:0 M:0 Y:0 K:56
R:146 G:146 B:146

C:0 M:100 Y:100 K:0
R:230 G:0 B:18

C:100 M:0 Y:100 K:0
R:0 G:153 B:68

C:0 M:0 Y:100 K:0
R:255 G:241 B:0

C:0 M:0 Y:0 K:23
R:215 G:215 B:216

C:0 M:33 Y:0 K:0
R:246 G:195 B:217

C:0 M:0 Y:93 K:0
R:255 G:241 B:0

C:0 M:0 Y:0 K:37
R:187 G:188 B:188

C:75 M:0 Y:100 K:0
R:34 G:172 B:56

C:0 M:0 Y:100 K:0
R:255 G:241 B:0

C:0 M:72 Y:20 K:0
R:235 G:104 B:140

C:0 M:0 Y:0 K:50
R:159 G:160 B:160

83

Key Visual Design Development

Studio: Coton Design
Designer: Hiroko Sakai

Idea: Bold color blocking

Key Visual Design Development is a design book that introduces many design cases presented through key visual designs. Because the subtitle is "Eye-catching Promotional Concepts", the designer used 2 lines of sight to present this theme and expressed the concept of "designs extend from the key visual" with simple figures. T&K TOKA, a Japanese ink company, provided 4 kinds of fluorescent ink to print this book. The inks used include TOKA FLASH VIVA DX 300 (red), TOKA FLASH VIVA DX 610 (yellow), TOKA FLASH VIVA DX 630 (green), and TOKA FLASH VIVA DX 850 (blue). All of these colors belong to the TOKA FLASH VIVA DX series. The red color in this series must be printed twice and shielded by polypropylene after printing to protect the color from abrasion. This kind of design in colors and composition is a representation of the contemporary "New Ugly" style.

C:12 M:0 Y:88 K:0
R:236 G:232 B:34

C:0 M:70 Y:35 K:0
R:234 G:89 B:115

C:02 M:21 Y:2 K:0
R:0 G:150 B:214

C:45 M:0 Y:87 K:0
R:156 G:202 B:67

84

We Are The Human Network

Studios: Bernstein & Andriulli Inc., Takeuma
Art Director: Giulio Nadotti

Idea: Creating psychological suggestions through colors

Advertising agency We Are The Human Network is a global independent communication agency with a humanized approach to business. It asked designers to create commercial images with themes like "Our People", "Our Network", "Our Customer", and "Our World". Orange is the brand color of the agency. The designers chose green to express the brand's sense of unity, progress, strength and trust. Both colors are full of vigor and vitality, indicating that the brand is moving forward and opening the door to a new world.

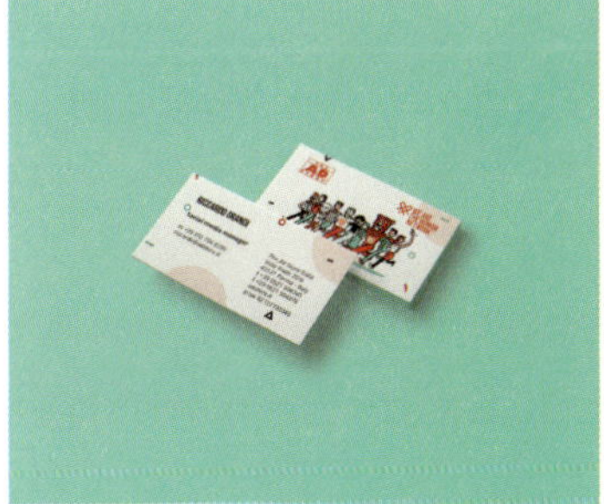

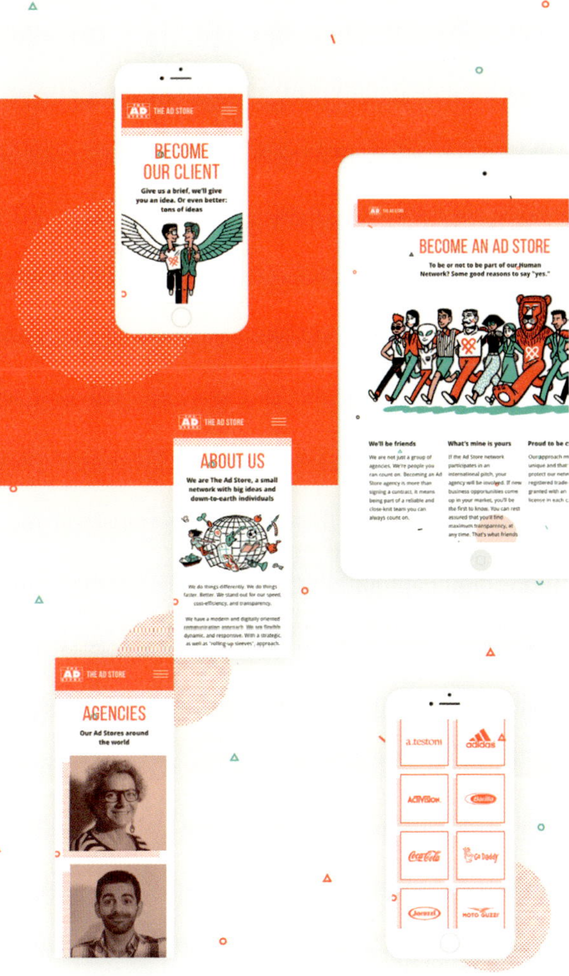

C:13 M:90 Y:93 K:0
R:213 G:57 B:33

C:59 M:0 Y:43 K:0
R:104 G:192 B:165

85

Fromhand Make Up Academy

Studio: Dentsu

Designer: Aya Yagi

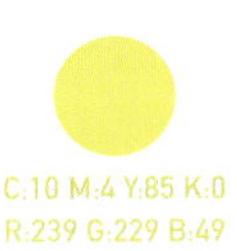

Idea: Large background with bright colors

This is an ad created for the beauty school Fromhand Make Up Academy. In order to highlight the fact that it is a beauty school, the models have had their hair styled in a variety of colors and shapes and linked to long handles to resemble make-up brushes. The font design combines English and Japanese characters to reflect the curriculum of the school. Bright background colors of red, yellow, blue and violet, complement each other and the charming models, creating a bold, avant-garde effect.

86

Works by Ryu Mieno

Designer: Ryu Mieno

Idea: Collision of muted colors

Ryu Mieno graduated from Kyoto Seika University and is now a freelance designer. His designs involve a wide range of elements. He is a member of the mural art team "uwn!" and is currently responsible for the design of *AT PAPER*. This series of graphic works features randomly cut compositions and collisions of dull, dark colors, creating a strong visual impact.

C:100 M:89 Y:4 K:0
R:8 G:51 B:141

C:100 M:0 Y:85 K:0
R:0 G:154 B:91

C:76 M:0 Y:37 K:0
R:0 G:177 B:175

「あの時代」と今日の美術。そして紙芝居、漫画、アニメ、特撮 ●● など。

Oh!マツリ★ゴト 昭和・平成のヒーロー&ピープル

Heroes and People in the Japanese Contemporary Art

2019年1月12日㊏ - 3月17日㊐

兵庫県立美術館
HYOGO PREFECTURAL MUSEUM OF ART

月曜日(ただし1月14日(月・祝)と2月11日(月・祝)は開館、1月15日(火)と2月12日(火)は休館)

午前10時－午後6時(金・土曜日は午後8時まで) ※入場は閉館の30分前まで

一般…1,300円(1,100)円 大学生…900(700)円 70歳以上…650(550)円 高校生以下無料

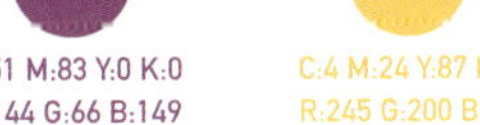

C:51 M:83 Y:0 K:0
R:144 G:66 B:149

C:4 M:24 Y:87 K:0
R:245 G:200 B:38

87

The Roasters and the Stand

Studio: Emuni
Designers: Masashi Murakami, Moe Shibata

THE ROASTERS AND THE STAND

COFFEE BEANS
WHOLE / GRIND

WE WANNA BE GOOD EXPERIENCE SUPPLIER. THAT IS AN IDEAL LIFE STYLE FOR US. WE ARE WORKING FOR GOOD PEOPLE, GOOD COFFEE.

Panama

C:0 M:69 Y:12 K:0
R:236 G:112 B:153

C:93 M:74 Y:2 K:0
R:17 G:74 B:156

C:0 M:0 Y:100 K:0
R:255 G:241 B:0

C:62 M:0 Y:16 K:0
R:83 G:192 B:214

C:26 M:69 Y:0 K:0
R:192 G:103 B:165

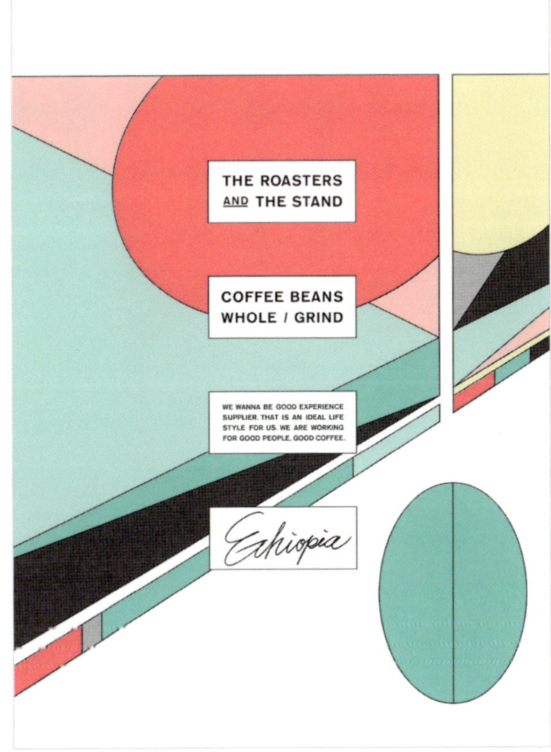

Idea: Color blocks collide to strengthen visual effect

Boutique coffee shop The Roasters roasts high-quality coffee beans according to the characteristics of the place of origin and ships them wholesale throughout Japan. The unique flavor and style of the beans are subtly transformed into colors and figures to express the iconic features of their countries of origin. Wrapping paper and bags are designed to represent the different countries, with patterns unifying the overall design style. The colors are cut into various irregular blocks and pieced together in a seemingly cluttered but eye-catching arrangement that defies the traditional rules of color matching.

CostaRica
WE WANNA BE GOOD EXPERIENCE SUPPLIER. THAT IS AN IDEAL LIFE STYLE FOR US. WE ARE WORKING FOR GOOD PEOPLE, GOOD COFFEE.
Indonesia
COFFEE BEANS WHOLE / GRIND
THE ROASTERS AND THE STAND
Brasil
THE ROASTERS AND THE STAND
COFFEE BEANS WHOLE / GRIND
Honduras
THE ROASTERS AND THE STAND
COFFEE BEANS WHOLE / GRIND

THE ROASTERS AND THE STAND
COFFEE BEANS WHOLE / GRIND
THE ROASTERS AND THE STAND
COFFEE BEANS WHOLE / GRIND
THE ROASTERS AND THE STAND
COFFEE BEANS WHOLE / GRIND

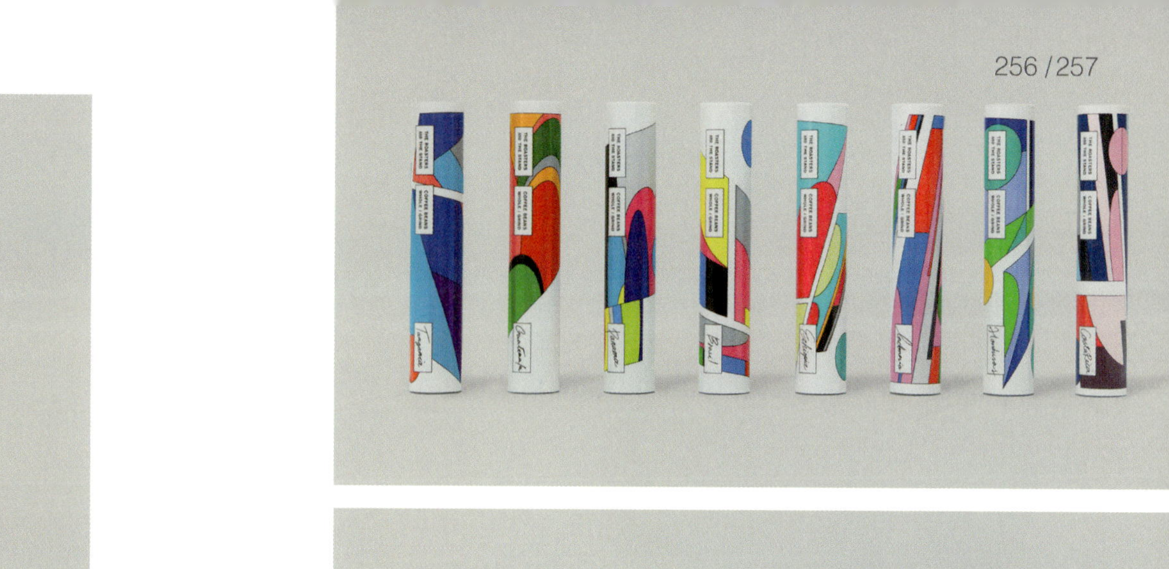

THE ROASTERS AND THE STAND
COFFEE BEANS WHOLE / GRIND
Honduras
THE ROASTERS AND THE STAND
COFFEE BEANS WHOLE / GRIND
Guatemala
THE ROASTERS AND THE STAND
COFFEE BEANS WHOLE / GRIND
CostaRica
THE ROASTERS AND THE STAND
COFFEE BEANS WHOLE / GRIND

THE ROASTERS AND THE STAND
COFFEE BEANS WHOLE / GRIND

88

Idea: Eye-catching fluorescent colors

Takuya Yamashita Exhibition

Designer: Takuya Yamashita

The Takuya Yamashita Exhibition adopted a collision of fluorescent colors for its publicity material. This type of design can effectively stimulate the eyes and give viewers a sense of being blinded by the bright colors if they look at it for an extended period of time.

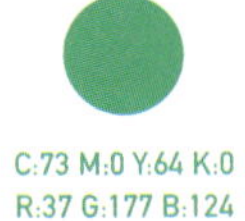

C:73 M:0 Y:64 K:0
R:37 G:177 B:124

C:0 M:87 Y:76 K:0
R:232 G:65 B:54

C:7 M:4 Y:86 K:0
R:255 G:240 B:0

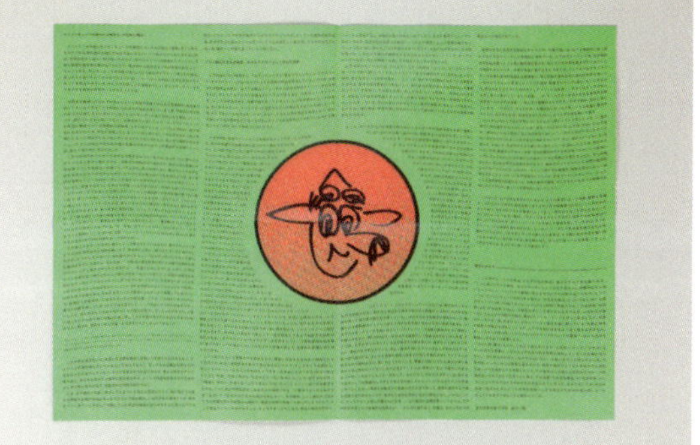

YAMASHITA TAKUYA
山下拓也

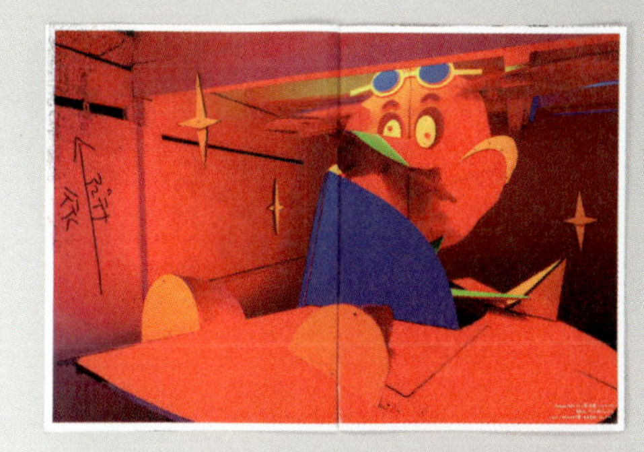

89

YOIGOMA

Studio: KIGI Co., Ltd.
Designer: Chisato Endo
Art Directors: Ryosuke Uehara, Yoshie Watanabe
Creative Directors: Satoru Miyata, Ryosuke Uehara

Idea: Rotating colorful patterns

YOIGOMA is a sake from Niigata Prefecture in Japan. The theme of the design is "drunk", so the designer used different colors to form rotating patterns on the packaging to imitate the interesting experience of dizziness after a person becomes drunk.

C:18 M:89 Y:33 K:0
R:204 G:56 B:109

C:82 M:6 Y:54 K:0
R:0 G:164 B:140

C:77 M:9 Y:8 K:0
R:0 G:168 B:217

90

ROOMBLOOM IFFT 2013 Booth Designs

Studio: Minna Inc.
Designers: Satoshi Hasegawa, Mayuko Tsunoda
Photographer: Kenta Hasegawa

C:95 M:73 Y:0 K:0
R:0 G:74 B:159

C:77 M:4 Y:6 K:0
R:0 G:174 B:225

C:7 M:68 Y:17 K:0
R:225 G:112 B:148

C:12 M:16 Y:60 K:0
R:231 G:211 B:120

C:26 M:20 Y:0 K:0
R:196 G:200 B:229

C:65 M:6 Y:36 K:0
R:81 G:181 B:174

Idea: Using plain background colors to emphasize the subject

As an interior paint brand owned by Nippon Paint Holdings, ROOMBLOOM has adopted "Repainting Life" as the title of its new booth design to show the connection between life and paint. In order to highlight the colorful and bright paint products, the background of the entire booth is white, making the various painted shapes brighter and more eye-catching.

91

Lumine Autumn Campaign "My Voice My Story"

Studio: POOL Inc.
Art Director: Etsuko Iwasaki

C:67 M:12 Y:0 K:0
R:61 G:174 B:228

C:7 M:0 Y:68 K:0
R:245 G:239 B:106

C:9 M:15 Y:15 K:0
R:235 G:221 B:213

Idea: Placid colors accentuate fluorescent blue

The designer was commissioned by Lumine to design showcases, signage and tapestries for 10 of its department stores in Tokyo for a month-long brand design exhibition. The designer considered the fashion preferences of women in their 20s to 30s during the creation process and highlighted the placid and peaceful autumn atmosphere in his work. The female characters in his design all feature large blue eyes, which the designer thought was very interesting as he does not usually use this kind of color.

92

Ryuko Tsushin

Designer: Kazunari Hattori

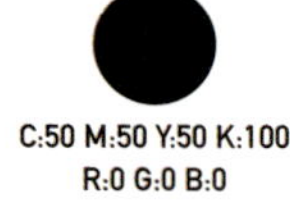

C:50 M:50 Y:50 K:100
R:0 G:0 B:0

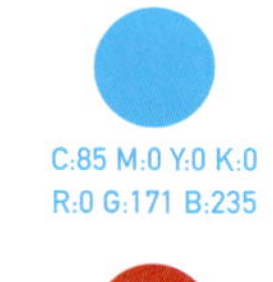

C:85 M:0 Y:0 K:0
R:0 G:171 B:235

C:0 M:0 Y:100 K:0
R:255 G:241 B:0

C:53 M:81 Y:7 K:0
R:140 G:71 B:145

C:14 M:100 Y:86 K:0
R:210 G:15 B:42

C:0 M:0 Y:17 K:0
R:255 G:253 B:225

Kazunari Hattori is a Japanese graphic designer and art director. He graduated from Tokyo University of the Arts in 1988 with a degree in design and entered Light Publicity, a Japanese advertising agency, the same year. He founded his own independent studio in 2001 and has worked as the print ads director for brands such as Kewpie Half and JR East Railway, and the art director for magazines such as *Ryuko Tsushin.*

Idea: Unusual choice in background colors

Ryuko Tsushin's new logo, which consists of square dots, has a digital style and slightly distorted strokes. In order to match the unconventional logo, the magazine cover also needs an individual color scheme. For example, the cover may feature a black background, which is not a common choice for other magazines, or the cover will feature a messy pile of books on a white background. Hattori wants to create a magazine that not only looks good, but also is fun to read.

minä perhonen koti

Studio: TORAFU ARCHITECTS
Creative Directors: Koichi Suzuno, Shinya Kamuro
Photographer: Takumi Ota

Idea: Messy but beautiful colors

This is the interior design for minä perhonen koti, a Japanese fashion brand. The "koti" in its name means "house" in Finnish, as the store mainly sells household goods such as cushions and tableware. A square section of the store floor is covered in colorful fabric and buttons secured with epoxy resin for customers to appreciate. The store seems to be chaotic and filled with a variety of products, but, in fact, each product and color is carefully matched by the designer and possesses specific variations.

Color Matching Reference

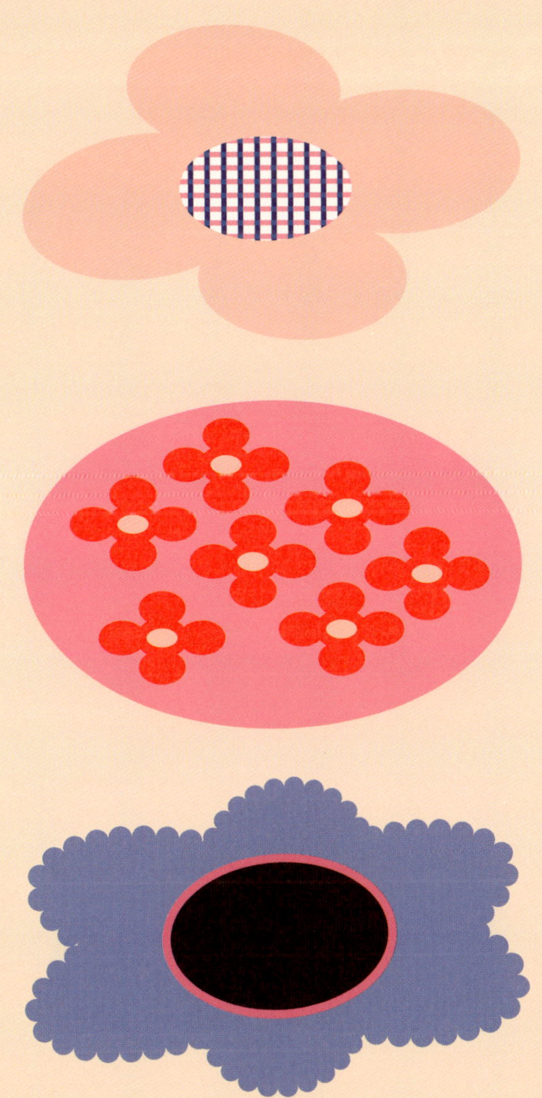

レトロセンス

Retro Sense

Bicolor Matching
ツートーンカラー

Tricolor Matching
3トーンカラー

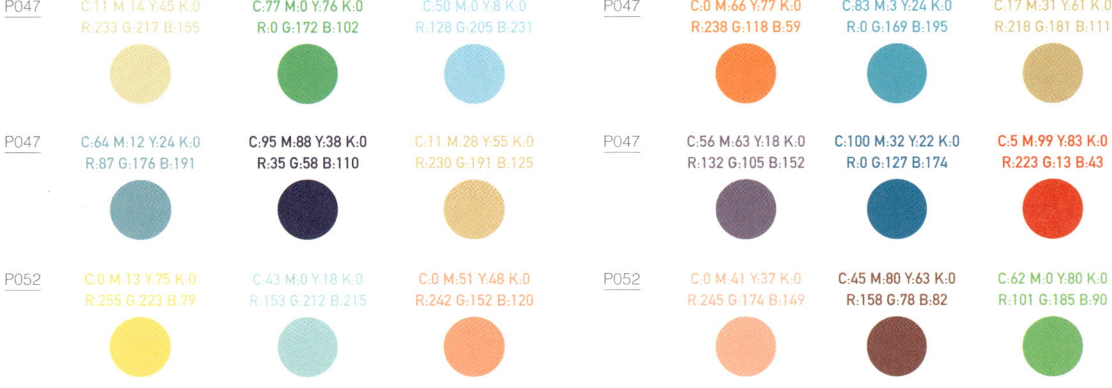

P052	C:0 M:92 Y:83 K:0 R:231 G:49 B:43	C:88 M:82 Y:0 K:0 R:54 G:62 B:150	C:34 M:0 Y:44 K:0 R:182 G:218 B:165
P052	C:0 M:13 Y:75 K:0 R:255 G:223 B:79	C:89 M:48 Y:0 K:0 R:0 G:111 B:186	C:34 M:0 Y:44 K:0 R:182 G:218 B:165
P059	C:38 M:25 Y:85 K:0 R:175 G:174 B:65	C:46 M:77 Y:75 K:7 R:150 G:80 B:66	C:9 M:19 Y:81 K:0 R:237 G:206 B:63
P074	C:30 M:2 Y:10 K:0 R:188 G:224 B:231	C:50 M:4 Y:74 K:0 R:141 G:193 B:99	C:10 M:95 Y:100 K:0 R:217 G:40 B:23
P075	C:0 M:0 Y:0 K:15 R:230 G:230 B:230	C:58 M:32 Y:15 K:0 R:118 G:154 B:188	C:20 M:82 Y:73 K:0 R:203 G:78 B:64
P076	C:50 M:35 Y:73 K:0 R:146 G:151 B:90	C:0 M:0 Y:0 K:30 R:201 G:202 B:202	C:5 M:9 Y:11 K:0 R:244 G:235 B:227
P088	C:100 M:65 Y:78 K:9 R:0 G:83 B:75	C:42 M:32 Y:42 K:0 R:163 G:164 B:147	C:2 M:27 Y:35 K:0 R:246 G:202 B:165
P089	C:100 M:55 Y:82 K:17 R:0 G:88 B:70	C:37 M:50 Y:96 K:0 R:177 G:134 B:38	C:0 M:0 Y:0 K:35 R:191 G:192 B:192
P091	C:95 M:30 Y:9 K:0 R:0 G:131 B:194	C:53 M:65 Y:71 K:7 R:135 G:98 B:77	C:16 M:0 Y:81 K:0 R:227 G:229 B:68
P091	C:0 M:97 Y:95 K:0 R:230 G:25 B:25	C:0 M:27 Y:97 K:0 R:251 G:196 B:0	C:99 M:75 Y:14 K:0 R:0 G:73 B:144
P096	C:71 M:9 Y:75 K:0 R:67 G:168 B:100	C:38 M:5 Y:74 K:0 R:175 G:204 B:95	C:0 M:80 Y:51 K:0 R:234 G:84 B:92
P097	C:70 M:16 Y:0 K:0 R:48 G:166 B:223	C:90 M:69 Y:0 K:0 R:26 G:81 B:163	C:71 M:66 Y:0 K:0 R:95 G:92 B:167
P097	C:36 M:99 Y:77 K:0 R:174 G:32 B:57	C:89 M:54 Y:58 K:7 R:2 G:100 B:103	C:19 M:57 Y:7 K:0 R:207 G:133 B:174
P106	C:58 M:40 Y:71 K:0 R:126 G:139 B:93	C:91 M:50 Y:82 K:33 R:0 G:83 B:59	C:30 M:30 Y:39 K:0 R:190 G:176 B:154
P106	C:52 M:74 Y:71 K:13 R:132 G:79 B:69	C:28 M:28 Y:38 K:0 R:195 G:181 B:158	C:72 M:69 Y:71 K:31 R:76 G:68 B:63

Four-color Matching

4トーンカラー

P061	C:0 M:100 Y:82 K:0 R:230 G:0 B:42	C:0 M:32 Y:16 K:0 R:247 G:195 B:194	C:7 M:7 Y:14 K:0 R:241 G:236 B:223	C:0 M:22 Y:86 K:0 R:253 G:206 B:39

P063
C:0 M:100 Y:100 K:0
R:230 G:0 B:18
C:100 M:100 Y:100 K:100
R:0 G:0 B:0
C:0 M:55 Y:95 K:0
R:241 G:141 B:2
C:0 M:20 Y:95 K:0
R:253 G:209 B:0
P065
C:0 M:94 Y:89 K:0
R:231 G:41 B:34
C:89 M:68 Y:0 K:0
R:30 G:83 B:164
C:93 M:45 Y:99 K:15
R:0 G:102 B:55
C:25 M:31 Y:63 K:0
R:202 G:176 B:107
P070
C:0 M:49 Y:27 K:0
R:242 G:158 B:157
C:54 M:51 Y:25 K:0
R:135 G:126 B:156
C:38 M:11 Y:78 K:0
R:175 G:195 B:84
C:81 M:36 Y:81 K:0
R:42 G:130 B:84
P070
C:31 M:3 Y:23 K:0
R:187 G:220 B:206
C:13 M:40 Y:81 K:0
R:224 G:166 B:62
C:60 M:22 Y:28 K:0
R:109 G:166 B:177
C:10 M:65 Y:85 K:0
R:223 G:117 B:47
P071
C:81 M:30 Y:25 K:0
R:0 G:140 B:173
C:54 M:16 Y:67 K:0
R:131 G:175 B:110
C:100 M:52 Y:82 K:18
R:0 G:90 B:70
C:7 M:20 Y:60 K:0
R:240 G:208 B:118
P072
C:20 M:96 Y:75 K:0
R:201 G:37 B:57
C:20 M:35 Y:35 K:0
R:210 G:175 B:157
C:44 M:8 Y:20 K:0
R:152 G:200 B:205
C:82 M:33 Y:54 K:0
R:11 G:134 B:126
P077
C:59 M:0 Y:17 K:0
R:97 G:195 B:213
C:95 M:0 Y:82 K:0
R:0 G:158 B:95
C:0 M:36 Y:43 K:0
R:247 G:184 B:142
C:0 M:58 Y:48 K:0
R:240 G:137 B:114
P079
C:100 M:46 Y:0 K:0
R:0 G:109 B:187
C:0 M:100 Y:100 K:0
R:230 G:0 B:18
C:0 M:0 Y:100 K:0
R:255 G:241 B:0
C:0 M:75 Y:92 K:0
R:235 G:97 B:27
P093
C:26 M:2 Y:28 K:0
R:200 G:225 B:198
C:41 M:38 Y:21 K:0
R:164 G:157 B:175
C:20 M:47 Y:36 K:0
R:208 G:152 B:144
C:18 M:22 Y:43 K:0
R:217 G:198 B:153
P093
C:40 M:51 Y:0 K:0
R:166 G:134 B:188
C:10 M:13 Y:29 K:0
R:234 G:222 B:189
C:53 M:71 Y:56 K:0
R:141 G:92 B:97
C:43 M:45 Y:79 K:0
R:163 G:140 B:74

Multi-color Matching
マルチカラー

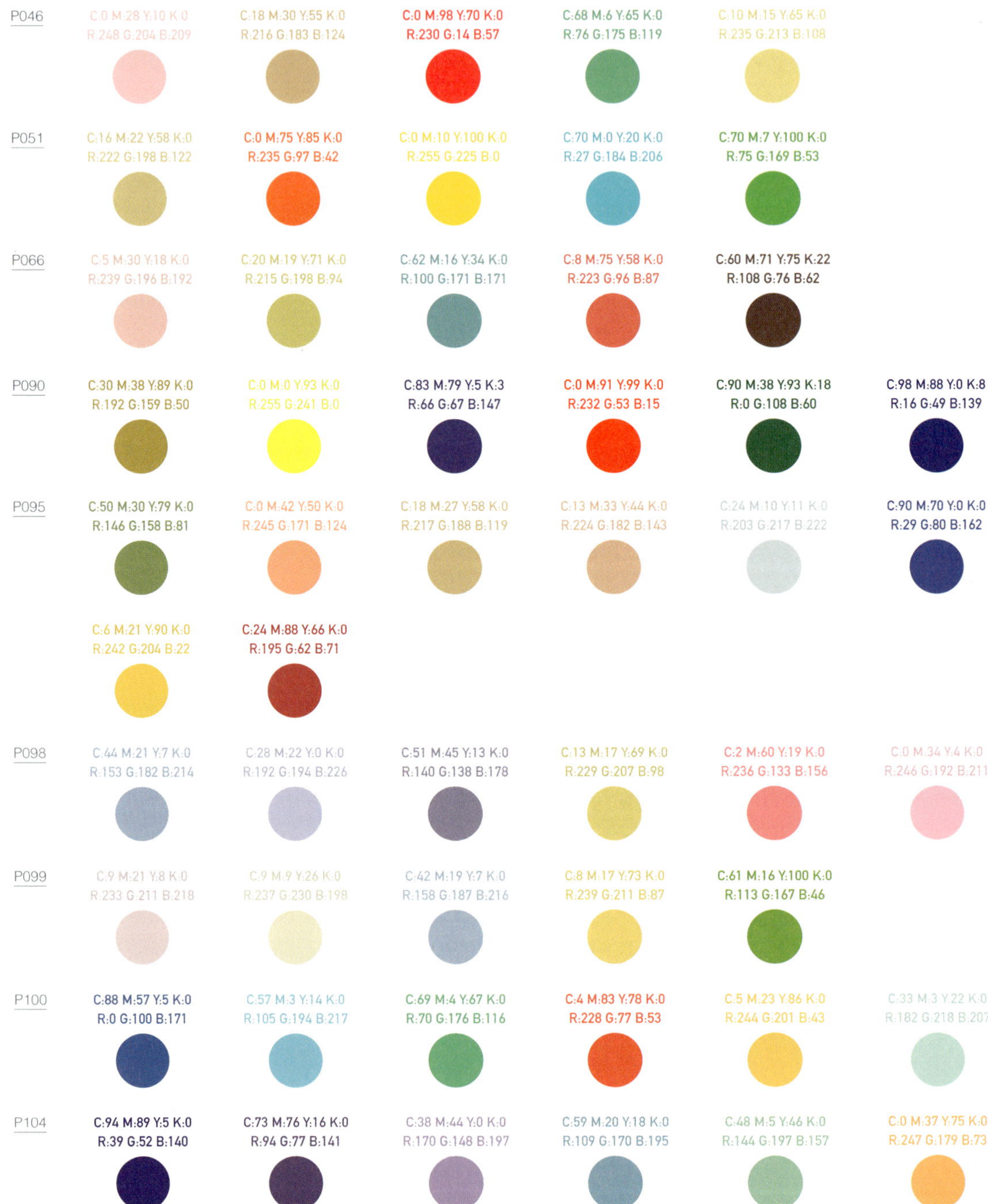

ミニマリズム
Minimalism

Monochrome
モノクロカラー

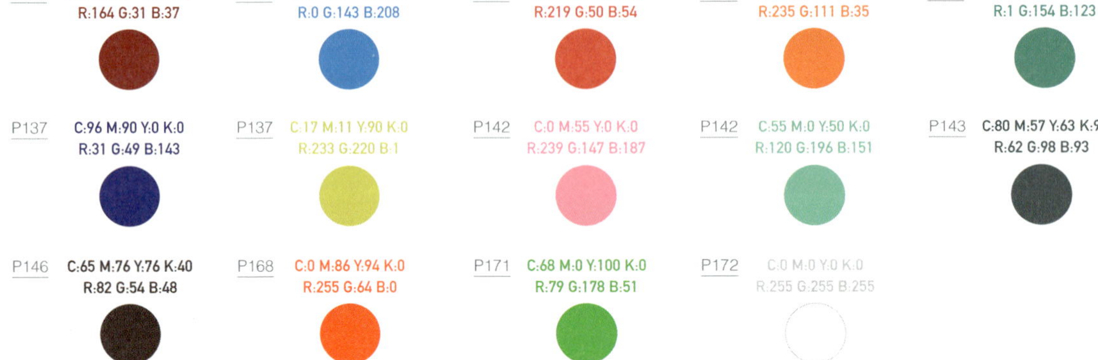

Bicolor Matching
ツートーンカラー

Tricolor Matching
3トーンカラー

P130	C:100 M:79 Y:8 K:0 R:0 G:66 B:146	C:48 M:22 Y:0 K:0 R:141 G:177 B:222 	C:78 M:15 Y:11 K:0 R:0 G:160 B:207 
P167	C:57 M:100 Y:87 K:49 R:87 G:0 B:24 	C:10 M:20 Y:20 K:0 R:232 G:211 B:199 	C:47 M:81 Y:100 K:14 R:146 G:69 B:21 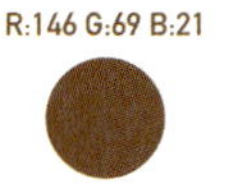

Four-color Matching
4トーンカラー

P112	C:9 M:79 Y:15 K:0 R:220 G:84 B:138 	C:65 M:0 Y:43 K:0 R:78 G:187 B:164 	C:54 M:70 Y:4 K:0 R:137 G:92 B:160 	C:17 M:9 Y:65 K:0 R:222 G:217 B:112 
P114	C:8 M:24 Y:31 K:0 R:236 G:203 B:175 	C:16 M:14 Y:35 K:0 R:222 G:214 B:175 	C:6 M:10 Y:8 K:0 R:242 G:233 B:231 	C:8 M:36 Y:28 K:0 R:232 G:181 B:169 
P117	C:0 M:0 Y:0 K:0 R:255 G:255 B:255 	C:74 M:20 Y:41 K:0 R:50 G:156 B:155 	C:48 M:10 Y:20 K:0 R:141 G:194 B:202 	C:0 M:71 Y:60 K:0 R:236 G:107 B:85 
P122	C:31 M:41 Y:71 K:0 R:189 G:154 B:88 	C:40 M:5 Y:15 K:0 R:162 G:209 B:217 	C:10 M:33 Y:18 K:0 R:229 G:186 B:189 	C:53 M:77 Y:0 K:0 R:139 G:78 B:155 
P139	C:29 M:33 Y:75 K:0 R:194 G:169 B:82 	C:46 M:18 Y:53 K:0 R:153 G:181 B:136 	C:13 M:55 Y:27 K:0 R:219 G:139 B:150 	C:80 M:73 Y:32 K:0 R:74 G:81 B:127 
P140	C:2 M:41 Y:0 K:0 R:241 G:177 B:206 	C:11 M:19 Y:26 K:0 R:231 G:211 B:189 	C:87 M:55 Y:4 K:0 R:3 G:103 B:175 	C:92 M:57 Y:100 K:34 R:0 G:75 B:41 
P140	C:2 M:41 Y:0 K:0 R:241 G:177 B:206 	C:0 M:97 Y:96 K:0 R:230 G:25 B:23	C:11 M:19 Y:26 K:0 R:231 G:211 B:189 	C:44 M:84 Y:100 K:12 R:149 G:65 B:34 

P145

C:16 M:54 Y:0 K:0
R:212 G:140 B:186

C:80 M:15 Y:28 K:0
R:0 G:158 B:180

C:77 M:72 Y:42 K:4
R:81 G:81 B:113

C:32 M:44 Y:67 K:0
R:186 G:149 B:94

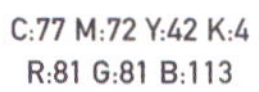

Multi-color Matching
マルチカラー

P110

C:10 M:15 Y:30 K:0
R:234 G:218 B:185

C:27 M:96 Y:100 K:0
R:190 G:41 B:32

C:0 M:16 Y:11 K:0
R:252 G:226 B:220

C:33 M:1 Y:10 K:0
R:184 G:228 B:237

C:38 M:22 Y:82 K:0
R:182 G:185 B:70

C:32 M:24 Y:20 K:0
R:185 G:188 B:193

P153

C:4 M:71 Y:54 K:0
R:230 G:106 B:95

C:6 M:30 Y:24 K:0
R:237 G:194 B:182

C:24 M:30 Y:43 K:0
R:203 G:180 B:147

C:44 M:53 Y:24 K:0
R:158 G:128 B:155

C:80 M:58 Y:78 K:23
R:57 G:86 B:66

C:29 M:0 Y:11 K:0
R:191 G:227 B:231

C:24 M:22 Y:87 K:0
R:206 G:189 B:53

P154

C:79 M:58 Y:71 K:15
R:64 G:92 B:79

C:67 M:0 Y:29 K:0
R:61 G:186 B:190

C:52 M:15 Y:5 K:0
R:127 G:184 B:222

C:16 M:32 Y:36 K:0
R:219 G:183 B:158

C:2 M:85 Y:61 K:0
R:230 G:71 B:76

P157

C:9 M:9 Y:11 K:0
R:236 G:232 B:226

C:25 M:54 Y:64 K:0
R:198 G:134 B:93

C:78 M:12 Y:83 K:0
R:17 G:159 B:87

C:8 M:53 Y:76 K:0
R:229 G:143 B:68

C:76 M:14 Y:9 K:0
R:0 G:163 B:211

C:20 M:98 Y:65 K:0
R:200 G:26 B:67

P161

C:65 M:10 Y:60 K:0
R:91 G:174 B:127

C:39 M:17 Y:67 K:0
R:177 G:192 B:107

C:10 M:10 Y:60 K:0
R:237 G:222 B:123

C:10 M:64 Y:58 K:0
R:222 G:120 B:94

C:65 M:23 Y:13 K:0
R:90 G:169 B:210

C:58 M:59 Y:12 K:0
R:130 G:115 B:172

C:0 M:60 Y:5 K:0
R:238 G:134 B:174

P163

C:10 M:52 Y:68 K:0
R:226 G:145 B:84

C:59 M:0 Y:25 K:0
R:99 G:194 B:199

C:5 M:55 Y:29 K:0
R:232 G:143 B:147

C:10 M:13 Y:82 K:0
R:237 G:215 B:61

C:68 M:59 Y:0 K:0
R:100 G:105 B:175

C:54 M:15 Y:0 K:0
R:119 G:182 B:228

C:50 M:60 Y:65 K:0
R:147 G:112 B:91

かわいらしさ

Kawaii

Monochrome
モノクロカラー

P188
C:50 M:4 Y:3 K:0
R:128 G:201 B:236

P212
C:54 M:94 Y:75 K:25
R:117 G:38 B:52

P212
C:85 M:54 Y:82 K:21
R:38 G:90 B:65

P212
C:90 M:80 Y:20 K:0
R:45 G:68 B:134

P212
C:14 M:17 Y:70 K:0
R:227 G:206 B:96

Bicolor Matching
ツートーンカラー

P211
C:74 M:76 Y:17 K:0
R:92 G:77 B:140

C:24 M:3 Y:75 K:0
R:208 G:219 B:89

Tricolor Matching
3トーンカラー

P178
C:2 M:30 Y:0 K:0
R:244 G:200 B:221

C:89 M:16 Y:0 K:0
R:0 G:151 B:220

C:69 M:0 Y:49 K:0
R:59 G:182 B:153

P180
C:6 M:98 Y:86 K:0
R:222 G:22 B:40

C:72 M:0 Y:55 K:0
R:39 G:178 B:141

C:6 M:22 Y:75 K:0
R:242 G:203 B:79

P184
C:65 M:12 Y:4 K:0
R:74 G:176 B:223

C:11 M:81 Y:0 K:0
R:216 G:77 B:150

C:57 M:73 Y:0 K:0
R:130 G:85 B:160

P187
C:80 M:41 Y:9 K:0
R:32 G:126 B:184

C:82 M:40 Y:100 K:0
R:45 G:124 B:58

C:10 M:9 Y:87 K:0
R:238 G:221 B:40

P191
C:10 M:31 Y:53 K:0
R:231 G:187 B:127

C:10 M:30 Y:0 K:0
R:229 G:194 B:219

C:10 M:13 Y:22 K:0
R:234 G:223 B:202

P192
C:76 M:43 Y:11 K:0
R:61 G:126 B:180

C:6 M:85 Y:31 K:0
R:223 G:68 B:114

C:7 M:55 Y:61 K:0
R:230 G:140 B:95

P196
C:0 M:0 Y:70 K:0
R:255 G:244 B:98

C:36 M:0 Y:34 K:0
R:175 G:217 B:185

C:35 M:20 Y:0 K:0
R:175 G:192 B:227

P196
C:0 M:20 Y:10 K:0
R:250 G:219 B:218

C:36 M:0 Y:34 K:0
R:175 G:217 B:185

C:0 M:0 Y:25 K:0
R:255 G:252 B:209

P196	C:0 M:0 Y:70 K:0 R:255 G:244 B:98	C:0 M:20 Y:10 K:0 R:250 G:219 B:218	C:50 M:0 Y:0 K:0 R:126 G:206 B:244
P197	C:0 M:20 Y:10 K:0 R:250 G:219 B:218	C:25 M:0 Y:10 K:0 R:200 G:231 B:233	C:35 M:20 Y:0 K:0 R:175 G:192 B:227
P203	C:0 M:11 Y:18 K:1 R:252 G:234 B:212	C:10 M:75 Y:100 K:83 R:71 G:11 B:0	C:0 M:15 Y:100 K:2 R:253 G:215 B:0
P203	C:0 M:15 Y:3 K:3 R:247 G:226 B:231	C:50 M:100 Y:0 K:60 R:80 G:0 B:71	C:0 M:15 Y:100 K:2 R:253 G:215 B:0
P204	C:10 M:0 Y:84 K:0 R:249 G:242 B:30	C:35 M:43 Y:51 K:0 R:182 G:151 B:123	C:44 M:50 Y:0 K:0 R:164 G:136 B:211
P219	C:78 M:21 Y:60 K:0 R:29 G:150 B:122	C:0 M:20 Y:70 K:0 R:253 G:211 B:92	C:0 M:83 Y:73 K:0 R:233 G:77 B:59

P197	C:0 M:0 Y:70 K:0 R:255 G:244 B:98	C:70 M:0 Y:60 K:0 R:58 G:180 B:131	C:35 M:20 Y:0 K:0 R:175 G:192 B:227
P200	C:9 M:0 Y:13 K:0 R:238 G:246 B:231	C:100 M:0 Y:100 K:77 R:0 G:60 B:11	C:0 M:15 Y:100 K:2 R:253 G:215 B:0
P203	C:14 M:0 Y:3 K:1 R:225 G:241 B:247	C:100 M:100 Y:0 K:22 R:23 G:23 B:118	C:0 M:15 Y:100 K:2 R:253 G:215 B:0
P204	C:36 M:0 Y:11 K:0 R:166 G:241 B:247	C:9 M:58 Y:51 K:0 R:234 G:138 B:113	C:58 M:0 Y:38 K:0 R:81 G:231 B:196
P215	C:0 M:95 Y:80 K:0 R:231 G:36 B:46	C:91 M:51 Y:71 K:12 R:0 G:99 B:85	C:7 M:24 Y:72 K:0 R:239 G:199 B:87

Four-color Matching
4トーンカラー

Multi-color Matching
マルチカラー

P179	C:2 M:30 Y:0 K:0 R:244 G:200 B:221	C:89 M:16 Y:0 K:0 R:0 G:151 B:220	C:69 M:0 Y:49 K:0 R:59 G:182 B:153	C:0 M:23 Y:68 K:0 R:252 G:206 B:96	C:0 M:85 Y:69 K:0 R:233 G:71 B:64		
P183	C:0 M:43 Y:35 K:0 R:244 G:170 B:150	C:0 M:85 Y:99 K:0 R:233 G:71 B:12	C:46 M:15 Y:56 K:11 R:142 G:172 B:122	C:57 M:2 Y:79 K:0 R:119 G:189 B:91	C:91 M:20 Y:3 K:0 R:0 G:145 B:212	C:7 M:23 Y:85 K:0 R:240 G:200 B:48	
P185	C:30 M:85 Y:87 K:0 R:194 G:72 B:49	C:76 M:13 Y:90 K:0 R:37 G:166 B:76	C:4 M:46 Y:91 K:0 R:247 G:162 B:17	C:0 M:52 Y:15 K:0 R:255 G:158 B:178	C:90 M:93 Y:13 K:0 R:61 G:48 B:138	C:38 M:73 Y:65 K:0 R:178 G:96 B:84	C:52 M:0 Y:33 K:0 R:132 G:210 B:194
P195	C:9 M:18 Y:88 K:0 R:238 G:207 B:36	C:9 M:87 Y:93 K:0 R:220 G:66 B:31	C:84 M:61 Y:55 K:15 R:48 G:87 B:97	C:15 M:30 Y:45 K:0 R:221 G:186 B:143	C:11 M:41 Y:88 K:0 R:227 G:165 B:42		
P207	C:14 M:29 Y:83 K:0 R:233 G:191 B:53	C:42 M:44 Y:0 K:0 R:170 G:149 B:224	C:44 M:27 Y:82 K:0 R:164 G:172 B:73	C:17 M:64 Y:29 K:0 R:220 G:123 B:143	C:60 M:36 Y:28 K:0 R:118 G:149 B:170		
P208	C:86 M:58 Y:34 K:0 R:36 G:100 B:136	C:73 M:52 Y:100 K:15 R:81 G:102 B:46	C:93 M:85 Y:58 K:34 R:27 G:45 B:69	C:10 M:20 Y:18 K:0 R:232 G:211 B:202	C:27 M:24 Y:17 K:0 R:196 G:191 B:198		
P209	C:59 M:65 Y:75 K:16 R:115 G:89 B:68	C:50 M:43 Y:40 K:0 R:145 G:141 B:141	C:19 M:33 Y:78 K:0 R:214 G:175 B:73	C:27 M:100 Y:99 K:0 R:189 G:26 B:34	C:73 M:48 Y:99 K:9 R:84 G:111 B:50		
P217	C:20 M:27 Y:93 K:0 R:214 G:183 B:27	C:0 M:82 Y:78 K:0 R:234 G:80 B:52	C:80 M:58 Y:0 K:0 R:59 G:101 B:176	C:66 M:0 Y:85 K:0 R:86 G:181 B:82	C:7 M:9 Y:86 K:0 R:244 G:223 B:42		

アバンギャルド

Avant-garde

Bicolor Matching
ツートーンカラー

Tricolor Matching
3トーンカラー

P238	C:0 M:100 Y:100 K:0 R:230 G:0 B:18	C:0 M:11 Y:22 K:0 R:254 G:234 B:205	C:100 M:69 Y:0 K:0 R:0 G:79 B:163
P241	C:0 M:0 Y:100 K:0 R:255 G:241 B:0	C:0 M:90 Y:0 K:0 R:230 G:46 B:139	C:100 M:0 Y:0 K:0 R:0 G:160 B:233
P244	C:38 M:0 Y:11 K:0 R:167 G:218 B:229	C:100 M:48 Y:0 K:0 R:0 G:107 B:185	C:0 M:95 Y:100 K:0 R:231 G:36 B:16
P245	C:100 M:0 Y:100 K:0 R:0 G:153 B:68	C:0 M:0 Y:100 K:0 R:255 G:241 B:0	C:0 M:0 Y:0 K:23 R:215 G:215 B:216
P245	C:0 M:33 Y:0 K:0 R:246 G:195 B:217	C:0 M:0 Y:93 K:0 R:255 G:241 B:0	C:0 M:0 Y:0 K:37 R:187 G:188 B:188
P252	C:100 M:89 Y:4 K:0 R:8 G:51 B:141	C:100 M:0 Y:85 K:0 R:0 G:154 B:91	C:76 M:0 Y:37 K:0 R:0 G:177 B:175
P258	C:73 M:0 Y:64 K:0 R:37 G:177 B:124	C:0 M:87 Y:76 K:0 R:232 G:65 B:54	C:7 M:4 Y:86 K:0 R:255 G:240 B:0
P261	C:18 M:89 Y:33 K:0 R:204 G:56 B:109	C:82 M:6 Y:54 K:0 R:0 G:164 B:140	C:77 M:9 Y:8 K:0 R:0 G:168 B:217
P264	C:67 M:12 Y:0 K:0 R:61 G:174 B:228	C:7 M:0 Y:68 K:0 R:245 G:239 B:106	C:9 M:15 Y:15 K:0 R:235 G:221 B:213
P267	C:50 M:50 Y:50 K:100 R:0 G:0 B:0	C:85 M:0 Y:0 K:0 R:0 G:171 B:235	C:0 M:0 Y:100 K:0 R:255 G:241 B:0

P267	C:53 M:81 Y:7 K:0 R:140 G:71 B:145	C:14 M:100 Y:86 K:0 R:210 G:15 B:42	C:0 M:0 Y:17 K:0 R:255 G:253 B:225

Four-color Matching

4トーンカラー

P228	C:3 M:40 Y:91 K:0 R:242 G:171 B:22	C:0 M:100 Y:100 K:0 R:230 G:0 B:18	C:71 M:14 Y:50 K:0 R:64 G:165 B:143	C:94 M:43 Y:5 K:0 R:0 G:116 B:186
P233	C:0 M:100 Y:0 K:0 R:228 G:0 B:127	C:100 M:0 Y:0 K:0 R:0 G:160 B:233	C:0 M:0 Y:100 K:0 R:255 G:241 B:0	C:0 M:0 Y:0 K:100 R:0 G:0 B:0
P237	C:25 M:19 Y:14 K:0 R:200 G:201 B:208	C:7 M:7 Y:7 K:0 R:240 G:237 B:236	C:71 M:14 Y:0 K:0 R:34 G:168 B:225	C:0 M:78 Y:67 K:0 R:234 G:90 B:70
P242	C:0 M:62 Y:50 K:0 R:238 G:128 B:108	C:0 M:10 Y:34 K:0 R:254 G:234 B:182	C:71 M:0 Y:45 K:0 R:41 G:181 B:160	C:0 M:29 Y:0 K:0 R:247 G:203 B:223
P243	C:68 M:32 Y:0 K:0 R:81 G:146 B:207	C:0 M:20 Y:0 K:0 R:250 G:220 B:233	C:29 M:0 Y:0 K:0 R:189 G:228 B:249	C:9 M:47 Y:100 K:0 R:230 G:153 B:0
P245	C:0 M:0 Y:100 K:0 R:255 G:241 B:0	C:75 M:0 Y:100 K:0 R:34 G:172 B:56	C:0 M:72 Y:20 K:0 R:235 G:104 B:140	C:0 M:0 Y:0 K:50 R:159 G:160 B:160
P247	C:12 M:0 Y:88 K:0 R:236 G:232 B:34	C:0 M:78 Y:35 K:0 R:234 G:89 B:115	C:82 M:21 Y:2 K:0 R:0 G:150 B:214	C:45 M:0 Y:87 K:0 R:156 G:202 B:67

Multi-color Matching
マルチカラー

P224	C:85 M:53 Y:0 K:0 R:20 G:106 B:181	C:0 M:76 Y:57 K:0 R:235 G:95 B:86	C:0 M:0 Y:0 K:20 R:220 G:221 B:221	C:24 M:0 Y:91 K:0 R:209 G:221 B:33	C:0 M:91 Y:16 K:0 R:230 G:45 B:123	C:73 M:0 Y:83 K:0 R:47 G:175 B:88
P225	C:0 M:0 Y:0 K:70 R:114 G:113 B:113	C:85 M:53 Y:0 K:0 R:20 G:106 B:181	C:0 M:91 Y:16 K:0 R:230 G:45 B:123	C:0 M:0 Y:0 K:20 R:220 G:221 B:221	C:24 M:0 Y:91 K:0 R:209 G:221 B:33	C:73 M:0 Y:83 K:0 R:47 G:175 B:88
P230	C:94 M:33 Y:8 K:0 R:0 G:128 B:192	C:0 M:46 Y:98 K:0 R:244 G:160 B:0	C:0 M:99 Y:88 K:0 R:230 G:8 B:35	C:79 M:38 Y:82 K:8 R:53 G:122 B:77	C:0 M:74 Y:3 K:0 R:234 G:99 B:157	
P231	C:69 M:6 Y:5 K:0 R:37 G:179 B:226	C:0 M:99 Y:98 K:0 R:230 G:8 B:20	C:0 M:58 Y:4 K:0 R:239 G:139 B:178	C:0 M:38 Y:92 K:0 R:247 G:176 B:9	C:81 M:30 Y:74 K:0 R:28 G:137 B:96	
P239	C:0 M:100 Y:100 K:0 R:230 G:0 B:18	C:100 M:0 Y:0 K:0 R:0 G:160 B:233	C:50 M:0 Y:100 K:0 R:143 G:195 B:31	C:0 M:35 Y:85 K:0 R:248 G:182 B:45	C:5 M:30 Y:45 K:0 R:240 G:193 B:143	C:0 M:21 Y:19 K:0 R:250 G:216 B:201
P243	C:0 M:53 Y:100 K:0 R:242 G:145 B:0	C:0 M:0 Y:85 K:0 R:255 G:242 B:38	C:57 M:0 Y:0 K:0 R:98 G:198 B:242	C:0 M:18 Y:0 K:0 R:251 G:224 B:236	C:0 M:100 Y:51 K:0 R:229 G:0 B:78	
P244	C:100 M:59 Y:0 K:0 R:0 G:93 B:173	C:0 M:71 Y:100 K:0 R:237 G:106 B:0	C:39 M:0 Y:100 K:0 R:173 G:206 B:0	C:95 M:0 Y:100 K:0 R:0 G:156 B:66	C:0 M:0 Y:0 K:56 R:146 G:146 B:146	C:0 M:100 Y:100 K:0 R:230 G:0 B:18
P254	C:0 M:69 Y:12 K:0 R:236 G:112 B:153	C:93 M:74 Y:2 K:0 R:17 G:74 B:156	C:0 M:0 Y:100 K:0 R:255 G:241 B:0	C:62 M:0 Y:16 K:0 R:83 G:192 B:214	C:26 M:69 Y:0 K:0 R:192 G:103 B:165	
P263	C:95 M:73 Y:0 K:0 R:0 G:74 B:159	C:77 M:4 Y:6 K:0 R:0 G:174 B:225	C:7 M:68 Y:17 K:0 R:225 G:112 B:148	C:12 M:16 Y:60 K:0 R:231 G:211 B:120	C:26 M:20 Y:0 K:0 R:196 G:200 B:229	C:65 M:6 Y:36 K:0 R:81 G:181 B:174
P269	C:10 M:26 Y:66 K:0 R:233 G:194 B:101	C:94 M:80 Y:0 K:0 R:25 G:64 B:152	C:62 M:0 Y:13 K:0 R:81 G:192 B:220	C:2 M:18 Y:0 K:0 R:247 G:223 B:236	C:47 M:0 Y:68 K:0 R:149 G:201 B:112	

Acknowledgements

We would like to thank all the designers and contributors who have been involved in the production of this book: their contributions have been indispensable to its creation. We would also like to express our gratitude to all the producers for their invaluable opinions and assistance throughout this project. And to the many others whose names are not credited but have made specific input in this book, we thank you for your continuous support.

Future Cooperations

If you wish to participate in SendPoints' future projects and publications, please send your website or portfolio to **editor02@sendpoints.cn**